EGYPTIAN SHAMAN

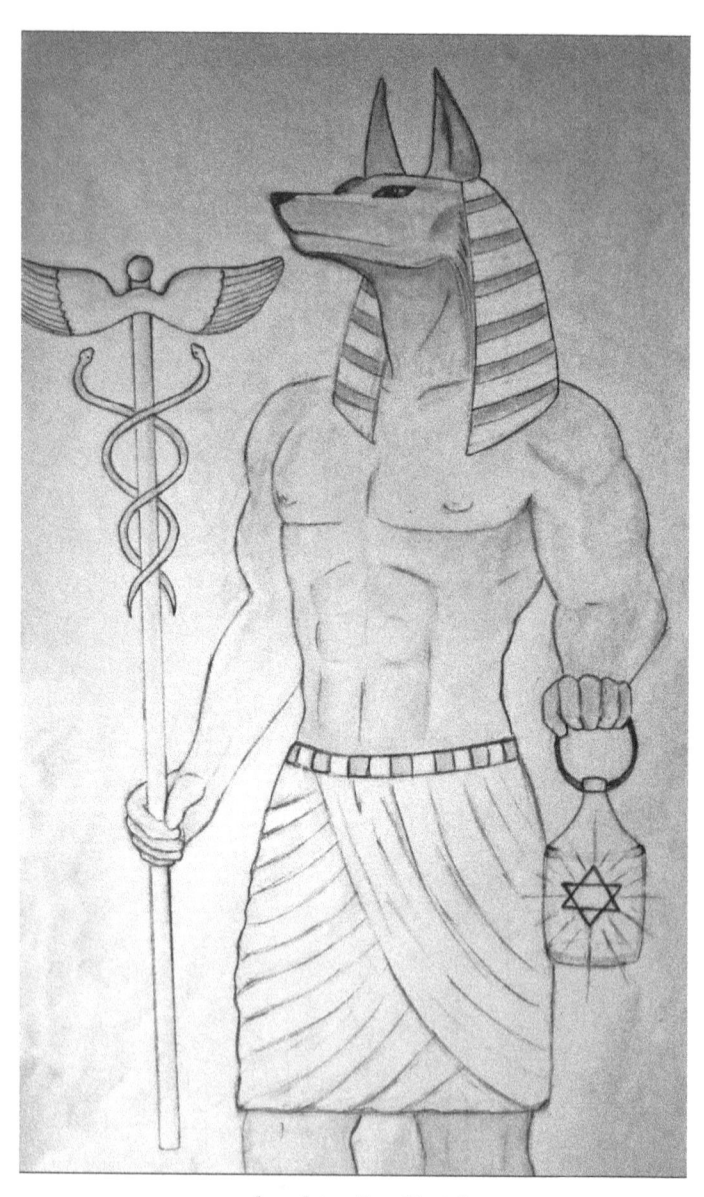

Anubis the Guide
By Paola Piacentini

Egyptian Shaman

Nick Farrell

MANDRAKE OF OXFORD

Other books by Nick Farrell

Making Talismans
Magical Pathworking
The Druical Order of Pendragon
Gathering the Magic: Creating 21st Century Esoteric Groups
Mathers's Last Secret
When a Tree Falls (Novel)

Work in Progress by Nick Farrell

The Golden Dawn Temple Tarot (with Harry Wendrich)
Mather's Torch
King over the Water

TO
DIDI TOTOMANOVA
AND
HER ILLUSTRIOUS ANCESTORS
AND
PAOLA FARRELL

Copyright © 2011 Nick Farrell

All rights reserved. No reproduction, copy or transmission of this publication may be made without written permission.
No paragraph of this publication may be reproduced, copied or transmitted save with the written permission or in accordance with the provision of the Copyright Act 1956 (as amended).
Any person who does any unauthorised act in relation to this publication may be liable for criminal prosecution and civil claims for damages.

The Moral Rights of the Author have been asserted.

A CIP catalogue record for this book is available from the British Library.

Cover design by

Paola Farrell

Printed and bound in Great Britain

Published by Mandrake
MANDRAKE OF OXFORD
PO Box 250
OXFORD
OX1 1AP (UK)

ISBN 978-1-906958-42-8

Web address www.mandrake.uk.net

Contents

Introduction	8
Chapter One The Time of the Shaman - Pre-dynastic Egypt	14
Chapter Two Shamans Ancient and Modern	44
Chapter Three Ancient Percussion and Chant	77
Chapter Four Animal Totems	102
Chapter Five The Ancestors	135
Chapter Six Exorcism	151
Chapter Seven Underworld Landscapes	178
Chapter Eight Healing and Magic	208
Chapter Nine Living the Life of an Egyptian Shaman	233
Appendix	246

INTRODUCTION

There are few systems of magic that have captured the imagination more than those credited to Ancient Egypt. From the early forms of Egyptian Freemasonry, to the elaborate rites of the Golden Dawn and the writings of Dion Fortune, Egypt has been at the forefront of the minds of the developers of the Western Mystery Tradition. But for all the power of these rites, few have looked at the texts left by the Ancient Egyptians and built a modern system based around them.

Notice that I have said build, not rebuild. I do not think it possible for any modern person to accurately re-create an Ancient Egyptian magic. An Ancient Egyptian was a different person, with dissimilar priorities and spiritual goals to a modern human. That which is a fable to us was concrete reality to them. To the Ancient Egyptians the sky was in reality a great river upon which the Sun god Re travelled, there was nothing symbolic about it! The Pharaoh was not a man who claimed to have the divine powers of a sun god, he embodied that deity on earth and Egyptians only accepted his or her rule on that basis.

Despite plenty of Ancient Egyptian religious and magical texts, we don't have a complete understanding about their beliefs. We forget the culture defined as Ancient Egypt was active for more than 3500 years. If you think about what we believe now and what our ancestors believed only 500 years ago, you should see how much variance there should be in Egyptian thought. Beliefs and religious practices varied between districts and villages and only in later times there was anything remotely like a 'unification' of belief.

In modern times only a few can accept the Sun as a living being, for the majority it can only be at best a symbol of the central spirit of life. To most, the Sun is just a ball of fiery gas, one of an infinite number of similar objects of different sizes floating around in the infinity of space in accordance to the laws of physics. Only the deranged would consider their politicians immortal Gods, even ranking them as human might be too kind.

This does not mean that Ancient Egypt has little spiritual to teach the modern person. Within the mindset of the Ancient Egyptian there were timeless spiritual truths. Symbols containing that truth describe inner and outer space. Readers of my book *Magical Pathworking* will be aware of the techniques used in building a personal inner kingdom using symbols to understand ourselves and the universe. In some respects this book is a companion to '*Magical Pathworking*, in that principles described there are used here.

Everyone builds around them an impression of reality – a unique image of the universe from their own perspective. Countless experiences build this universe. These are the lessons that we have taught ourselves or accepted as gospel from our parents, teachers, friends and society.

Occultism teaches that such a mental picture of the universe is such a powerful force for stability that it creates the circumstances to preserve it. In other words how we see our universe becomes a self-fulfilling prophecy.

Universes, built by the imagination, can be changed at will. The Ancient Egyptians created several elaborate inner kingdoms. Written in several symbolic books, which belong to various historic periods and world views, they provide a guide to life after death. The symbols contained in these books give an understanding of the worlds above and as well as the worlds below. More than one Egyptologist has suggested that it is likely these books might reflect initiations carried out by an elite while they were alive. Even if historically this is untrue, with some adaptations, they can still be powerful tools to initiation.

These texts provide a gloss over earlier 'shamanic' techniques. The texts read like descriptions of trance, inner world journeying, guides, totems and communication with spirits and the dead.

The term 'Shaman' also needs clarification. Shaman used to mean something specific. Shamans, or the female equivalent Shamana, were the magical spiritual leaders of Siberian people. For obvious reasons if we use this specific definition, it would be impossible for Shamans to have ever existed in Ancient Egypt. But over recent years the term Shaman has lost its association its male and original

Introduction

literal meaning. It has come to mean a proto-organised religion based around a spiritual leader who works magic using ecstatic trance. Victorian anthropologists and missionaries used this term to cover those cultures whose spiritual leaders were 'witch doctor' or more charitably 'medicine man'.

Egypt had these 'shamans' in its earliest period. As religion became more ordered and temple based, shamanic teaching and beliefs were absorbed. However, they can still be found. At a village level it is likely that their role was taken over by the magician, who can be seen muttering spells to help people fall in love in the modern era. The Ancient Egyptian priesthood also adopted some of their shamans' underworld roles. The expert in dealing with the Underworld in the later Egyptian temples was the Sem Priest, who still wore the animal skin of the shaman. We see them in Egyptian artwork in the role of communicating with the dead and guiding them through the Underworld. This role, which assumed much of the work of the ancient shaman and was in use until the collapse of the religion in Late Roman times.

It is impossible to say in any detail what methods or training the Sem-Priests used, or if they would be practical for modern minds. However, we can have a reasonably good guess and look to more modern developments to develop a spiritual path based on Ancient Egyptian beliefs. Modern neo-pagans have developed techniques from various native traditions and these are effective at accessing the symbols used by the Ancient Egyptians and I have adapted them in developing this.

I have mined from different parts of Egyptian culture to re-create a shamanic system that can be used by modern minds. What is interesting for me, as an experimenter, is there is a marked difference between the energy of the Egyptian shamanism and other shamanic 'traditions'. Ancient Egypt was a settled population from an early time. Its shamanic priesthood reflects agriculture, rather than the symbols of the hunter-gatherer cultures. It has more in common with modern neo-shamanic practices than it does with say, native American-based shamanism. It is more urban in its outlook, but, nature has a strong influence on it. Humanity and the mind have a greater part to play. It is a religion where nature had not been forgotten, as it was later, but was not overwhelming as it was much earlier. It is easier for modern minds to approach. Although the fears of the Ancients are with us, they do not overwhelm us because our rational mind is permitted to take part.

The goal of this book is to use the symbols of the Ancient Egyptians to achieve psychological integration, to lighten the dark places of the soul and to realise our spiritual sun within. It is designed to help serve your community, in the same way as a village magician. This means healing, negotiating with the spirits, working with the ancestors. It is a life journey of transformation for you, your family and community.

This book also contains many of the techniques that I have been taught by David Goddard, Samuel Robinson, and several others (who will wish to remain nameless) and put into practice. There will be some who will be deeply shocked that I have written about 'hard' issues such as exorcism and dealing with the dead. But these were important to Ancient Shamans and should be as important to those who follow this path today.

Dr Ron Hutton, who studied the beliefs of the Siberian Shaman, said that a person was called to the path by the spirits. Usually this was terrifying for them, because they would have to be dealing with the dead and their own fears daily. These people had teachers who would act as guides. Many modern shamans have only books and these contain watered-down Native American traditions, sweat lodges and drumming. Those who feel the ancient spirits calling them need something more than burning sage grass and drumming to follow the shamanic path. If they are going to find their Re (Sun) divine self and arise like a winter sun warming the spiritually chilled universe, they need techniques that can do that. So, this book includes information that will be valuable for those who approach Ancient Egypt from a ceremonial perspective.

Finally I would like to thank a few people who helped me to get all my ideas together. Alan Richardson and the late Billy Walker-John

Introduction

who got me thinking years ago about Inner Egypt. Marian Green who started me on the path of experimental magic and Samuel Robinson, who helped me understand some of the ideas behind the Maori tradition. I would also like to thank the Late David Williams, who besides being one of the few 'real' priests of Anubis I have met, helped me get my facts right when I insisted on using Budge's spelling. His partner Krys helped with the manuscript and, with her knowledge of Egypt, restored the Duck totem to its rightful place. Finally I would like to thank Donata Ahern, who has Inka and Huichol shamanic lineage and helped clarify a lot of my ideas.

This book was written nearly nine years ago and languished on my computer, circulated in a private manuscript and placed in "the coming soon" catalogue of a publisher for many years before I got it back. Thanks to Mogg Morgan for resurrecting this particular Osiris for me.

To all those who directly or indirectly helped, may you rise with Re in the boat of Millions of Years.

Nick Farrell
Rome
August 2011

Chapter One

The Time of the Shaman ~ Pre-dynastic Egypt

When thousands of workers dragged the stones of the Great Pyramid into place, they were making a statement of an advanced civilisation. It was a civilisation that had probably moved to the banks of the Nile more than 3,000 years earlier and changed from a simple tribal village culture to one which built cities that were the envy of the known world.

Such a world had for its spiritual backbone a long history of what today we call shamanism. The animal gods, such as the hawk, the jackal, the snake, worshipped as totem animals in these villages, did not disappear. Instead their myths and natures and even bodies became more human and intricate. When many Ancient Egyptians heard the harps and drums of the elaborate rites of Amun conducted in the great temples of Karnak, it was possible to hear the beat of drum of the pre-dynastic shaman.

In our search to hear this drum, to understand the role of the Egyptian shaman, build possible techniques and make it live for us, we have to go back to Egypt before the pyramids. It is the thousand year period called by early Egyptologists pre-dynastic because it was before Egypt a single Pharaonic dynasty unified the country.

The Time of the Shaman

Stone Age Egypt

There were Neolithic hunter and gathers in the Nile Delta area from 50,000BC. They would visit from the grasslands that were later to become the Sahara Desert. The Nile was not a habitable region then. The land was a dangerous mixture of lagoons, swamps and marshes. It was swarming with crocodiles, hippopotamuses, snakes and scorpions. On top of this for three months of the year the Nile flooded sweeping away everything that stood in its way.

It is uncertain when settlement in Egypt began. Suggested dates start at 25,000 BC, probably as the desert sands crushed life from the Sahara. By the fifth millennium there was a thriving culture along the Nile.

The people drove away the wild animals and the same flood made the area fertile for agriculture. Soon, the early Egyptians saw the yearly flood as a gift from the gods and the village heads had the religious duty of making sure it happened.

The culture was the Badarian, named after the village where archaeologists noted its first appearance. It was originally a nomadic culture that returned to the Nile periodically to grow crops. This culture dominated Egypt between 5,500 and 4500BC. Later, hunting for food declined as agricultural use developed and the people became settled. Their oldest settlement found so far has been at Beni Salamis on the western edge of the Delta. This town shows a degree of urbanisation as early as 4750BC. These people's religion is unknown, but it is possible the large number of female figures they worshipped a Goddess or several goddesses. There was a similar culture in the North of Egypt identified by Egyptologists as the Faiyum. The only difference between the two was the Faiyum were hunters. Both cultures buried their dead in the desert, because they did not want to waste good farmland.

They wrapped their dead in a reed mat and buried them. Sometimes the body was placed in a box or wickerwork coffin. Each body was laid in a fetal position on its left side with its hands near the face. In the graves were earthenware pots that contained food, which shows they believed the dead needed some symbolic nourishment in the afterlife. Some graves contain human figures which could be the prototype for the ubshabi figures and provided the dead with workers in the afterlife. Pre-dynastic graves contained flint tools, although it is not certain if these were for the dead person, or the workers.

The most important innovation of this period is the agriculture, which produced a chain of transformations of society. These include craftsmanship and rapid population growth.

Some chiefs, shamans or mixtures of both, could have begun to emerge as leaders of the groups. But the burials show no social difference and, during this time, the population was tribal.

Villages made a much greater impact on their environment. Archaeologists have found burned wood, animal skeletons, and remains of basic engineering projects including megaliths, temples and dykes.

Religion became more sophisticated with the objects connected religion being found. These proto-Egyptians did not try to preserve the dead. There are some graves where it is clear they scraped the skeleton free of flesh before burial.

It is clear the proto-Egyptians had a strong belief in the afterlife, however there is little sign they considered it a place where ordinary people went when they died. The graves suggest that such a future existence was the lot of chiefs and people of rank.

During the Fifth Millennium BC Egyptian Neolithic societies changed probably because a cultural or racial crossover between the local inhabitants of the Nile valley and Westerners.

By 4500 these Badarian and Faiyum cultures changed into the Amratian period. Amratian culture was advanced technologically and culturally, but worked alongside the Badarian culture for a while until it absorbed it.

Amratian graves contain depictions of totem animals, ivory magic wands with pendants of bearded men. Egypt was more agriculturally focused. Some archaeologists think statues of a bearded God are the first representations of Ausar the God of death, rebirth and agriculture others see him as representations of the god of fertility Amsu.

There is the earliest trace of the presence of grave goods in some burials, and an unseen before degree of social division.

In 4000 BC there was a huge technological and social change across Egypt into what is now dubbed the Gerzean period. Initially Egyptologists found the changes so dramatic that they suggested an invasion of an unknown 'desert people' from the East, possibly bringing their sun god Re with them.

One occult tradition says it was the period there was a migration fleeing a sinking Atlantis brought that land's technology, the bee, wheat, to Egypt. Pharaoh Ausar and his wife Aset were the first leaders.

The changes have happened in the North of Egypt first, however there is no archaeological evidence that an invasion or a migration took place and it appears the Gerzean changes were an Amratian evolution. All the changes were ideas that existed already within the culture.

It is in the Gerzean period, we see pictures of Gods riding in boats, or carrying totem animals on standards. There was a social division of society, particularly in death. For the rich there were underground tombs which look like fully furnished rooms, made of mud-brick. The tombs contained amulets and figures to act as workers in the afterlife. Painted on the walls were scenes with lions, bulls, hippopotamuses and falcons. The poor had oblong tombs with ledges where the bodies were lain.

Archaic Period

The Archaic Period is an arbitrary division of Egyptian History. It was only recently that Egyptologists thought of giving a name. It was almost identical with dynastic times that had failed to get a mention in the Egyptian records. Rather than mess around with the dating they invented a period between pre-dynastic and dynastic. Sometimes they called it Dynasty 0 and even suggest an earlier royal period called Dynasty 00.

When they look at the pre-dynastic period the Ancient Egyptians said that before the Pharaohs, the Followers of Heru or the Shemsu

Hor ruled the land. Heru was one of the earliest gods to be worshipped and later there are stories of this God's war with the Followers of Set (the Smayu Net Set). The Shemsu Hor description implies they were the names of the Kings of the Nomes in the North of Egypt. These took a "Heru name" when they took office. A drawing of their totem animal was put beside this Heru name on official documents.

We know the names of some of these rulers because the Egyptians invented writing around 3300BC. There were 17 of these Kings of whom we know only seven. They were: Heru Crocodile, Heru Hat-Hor, Heru Iry-Hor, Heru Ka, Heru Scorpion and Heru Baleful Catfish.

Later legends about the wars of Heru against Set (see Magical Pathworking) are more likely to be a myth to describe unifying Upper and Lower Egypt which took place between 3150 and 3110 BC. Heru was from the North and Set the south. During the pre-dynastic period Set was not the 'baddie' as he was in pre-dynastic times and was on the side of Re attacking the serpent of evil and darkness Apep.

Traditionally the first person to unite Egypt under its first Pharoah was Narma or 'Baleful Catfish'. However there is some proof the Heru Scorpion managed to do it much earlier. Some historians are now leaning toward the idea that unifying Egypt was not just a military conquest, but a gradual assimilation of the North by the South carried out over a long period of time.

The Gods in Pre-dynastic Egypt

Pre-dynastic Egyptians worshipped animals, birds, fish, reptiles and the powers of nature alongside human or part human gods. They believed that nature was the result of beings which could be unfriendly to humanity. When something bad happened that was the result of an unseen spirit working against them. A friendly spirit could bring good. There were spirits in the Air, in the mountains, streams and trees which needed respect and asked for help from the dangers that surrounded them.

These spirits were all grouped under the word Neteru.

The Time of the Shaman

Unfortunately for the last 200 years scholars have disagreed with what the word means. The hieroglyph of the word could be a flag on a pole, spread out by the wind. This gives the image of an inanimate object given movement by an unseen force. Another idea touted by earlier Egyptologists, such as Budge[1], the hieroglyph is of an axe[2]. The word means God, but the hieroglyph suggests the idea of 'power' as the axe was a symbol of a weapon and what the Ancient Egyptians used to carve out their domination of the Nile valley.

The pre-dynastic Egyptians believed the earth was overflowing with Neteru. Such beings, although invisible, were real and had the same range of emotions as humans. To make matters more complex, each part of a human had a Neteru assigned to it.

They believed that any spirit would grant a representation of itself with its power provided you knew its name. A spirit could live in a drawing or statue.

In this way all of nature was animate. However there was a divine hierarchy for life. The spirit in charge of the Nile was much bigger than that which was responsible for making a flower grow.

There was a duality between the different spirits. Beings that were always harmful to humanity were evil, while those that were more benign were good. If good spirits were treated with respect they would aid humanity. Respect meant acknowledgment of their power and offerings and worship. It is likely that it was these became as totem gods or animals.

The commonest form that a spirit made itself visible was in the form of an animal, bird, fish or reptile. According to Budge many Egyptians thought that animals had motives and passions similar to humans. Some animals, he claimed, had superhuman intelligence and the ability to talk. Budge's evidence is flimsy (he quotes what could be the equivalent of Egyptian children's stories), but could be indicative of the conversations with animal spirit guides common to many shamanic cultures.

A totem god or animal held the job for as long as the spirit helped

---

[1] The Gods of the Egyptians, WA Wallis Budge, Open Court, Chicago, 1904, p75
[2] The Hieroglyph for Heka, means magical power but can also mean leader.

the tribe or the village. Only a dominant god would survive when a village merged or was exterminated by war. Pictures of battle scenes show Totem poles carried into war, much like the flags in a modern army. Totem poles were present at important tribal gatherings. The problem was that a rival village could carry them off and take its power with them. If any harm came to the totem pole, the God or Goddess it represented would suffer.

Town or village's adopted older gods into their culture. When a person left a village and settled in another he sometimes took his gods with him, but would have to recognize the new ones.

Even as late as the Ptolomaic period, popular worship of the great national gods still featured totem animal symbolism.

Temples became bigger and more impressive. Large tree trunks supported the temple of Heru at Nekan. In other towns and villages temples were more modest. There worship of the local totem animal, tree or took place in a rounded God house. Later square or rectangular temples appear. Unlike ordinary houses temples had an opening which served as a doorway. During a later period such temples of mud-brick and had doorways with large wooden lintel. There were niches for a statue of the god.

Each place or tribe had its sacred animal. Worship of an animal sometimes took place and a representative would be cared for in the temple. After a given time, a priest killed the animal and its meat the tribe sacramentally ate its meat. This was the case with the Apis bull at Memphis and the ram at Thebes.

Where possible, the Ancient Egyptians tried to preserve their totem animals. Penalties for killing them were severe. In Dynastic times there were burial rites and mummification for totem animals.

From the earliest periods the most sacred animals were the snake, hawk, lion and scorpion. Egyptologists found totem animal statues in home and temple ruins and on talismans. Other sacred animal gods include hippopotamus, jackal, dog, duck, shrew mouse, vulture, ibis, goose, swallow, crocodile, frog, and cobra. It is uncertain if many of the various fish considered sacred including the oxyrhynkhos, phagros, lepidotos, latos ever made it to totem animal status, however insects such as the dung beetle, the cricket and the locust did.

There is some evidence of composite gods made of several different animals. One such being was Setcha who had the body of a leopard and the head and neck of snake. Another, Sefer, had the body of lion, and the wings of and head of an eagle.

It is possible the Ancient Egyptians believed in such creatures, in much the same way that Ancient Greeks believed that people in the East had one foot and mouths in their stomachs. However it is more likely the Egyptians are trying to capture the essence of different totem animals in a single picture. For example putting a human head on a leopard's body would give it human intelligence with the Leopard's speed.

After time the worship of animals reduced and their various qualities become incorporated in Gods that look like humans. The baboon became the emblem of Tahuti, the god of wisdom. Symbolically, the lion became Sekhmet, Bastet, Mahes, and Tefnut. Het-hor (the cow totem) took over cheetah and serval totems. Bastet claimed the cat totem and the bull taken by Apis and Ptah. The ram became Ausar, Hershefi, Amon, and Khnumu.

The head of the totem animal was attached to a human body making for a common god form. It is possible the idea came from shamans who might have worn masks of their gods while performing ceremonials.

Important in our period is Sokar, who was an early death God and later replaced by Ausar. He was a mummified hawk and he journeyed to the Underworld in a boat filled with hawks who were the spirits of dead kings. His name means silence and he had a wife Merteseger whose name means 'lover of silence'. He was less friendly than Ausar and in later periods was so scary that those entering his kingdom avoided him and his pyramid where he brooded in darkness.

One of the creator gods, Khnumu, made humanity on his potter's wheel. He had a ram's head and started out life as a Nile god who guarded the yearly flood.

Another 'animal god' who became anthropomorphic was Tehuti, was the god of writing, magic and earning. He had the head of an ibis and in one legend was one of the first gods to emerge from the primeval chaos. He represents the Divine consciousness which is behind creation.

Other animal gods or goddesses were Mentu (hawk), Sebek (crocodile), Heqt (frog), Hershefi (ram), Set (anteater), Anu (jackal) and Heru (hawk).

During the Gerzean period we first find mentioned 'human' Gods who will become important during the later Pharonic period.

Ausar is the most important and one of the oldest and reaches to the prehistoric age. It is likely that Ausar was a corn god connected to the cycle of birth and death. The planting and germination of the seed, the death of the seed, the birth of the barley, the death of the barley. He soon became the God of the Dead and he might have replaced Anu, who later became his son. It was to his kingdom the dead would live after death. According to legend, Ausar was a civilising king of Egypt. Murdered by his brother Set and seventy-two conspirators, sealed in a tree or wooden coffin and rescued by the magic of Astet (or Nebt-Het).

Aset (or Nebt-Het), his wife, found his coffin in Syria and brought it back to Egypt. Set tore up the body of Ausar and scattered it. Aset sought the fragments joined them and resurrected him long enough to produce a son – Heru. Aset and Heru then attacked Set and drove him from Egypt.

Dismembering Ausar and scattering of his body might go back to a period in Egyptian history where a king was sacrificed, cut up and buried in separate fields to ensure fertility. Budge suggests that Ausar was the god of a tribe which occupied a large part of Egypt during the pre-dynastic times. After thirty years' reign, like the ritual killing kings at fixed intervals elsewhere, the kings of this tribe became Ausar. The people ate his flesh ceremonially and his bones were spread among the 14 centres of the tribe with the head going to Abydos.

Nebt-Het, Nebt-het might have been an Aset prototype as her name, "mistress of the palace," suggests that she was Ausar's consort but Aset took her role . Known as the Sister of Aset the pair were

"The Two Ladies" who flanked the dead king on many coffins. She represents death, and decay. In later times she became the mother of Anu because of an affair with Ausar. This could be a hint the family of death made up of Ausar, Aset and Heru replaced an earlier family comprised of Anu, Nebt-Het and Ausar.

Aset became attached early on the Ausar worship; and appears in later myths as his sister and wife of Ausar. Her worship and priesthood were far more popular than those of Ausar, during a later period. Linking Heru to her myth, and making Aset a mother goddess, was the main reason for her importance in Greek and Roman times. However during our period, there was no focus on her mother attributions which was the role of Het-hor.

Heru: Heru, Hor, or Horu is an old and complicated God. We have already met him in his hawk form but he had many others. The first was the elder or greater Heru, Hor-ur. He was the brother of Ausar, older than Aset, Set, or Nebt-Het.

He was depicted in human form and could have been an early sky god. The other is the hawk-god of the south, who fights Set. Next there is Heru the sun god who has the winged solar disk as the emblem of Heru of Edfu, and the title of Heru on the horizons-- at rising and setting—Hor-emakhti. Then there is Heru of the two eyes; which represented both the sun and the moon. There is Heru the conqueror who appears as the hawk standing on the sign of gold, nub, nubti was the title of Set. Finally there is Hor-pe-khroti, "Heru the child." As the son of Aset he constantly appears from the nineteenth dynasty onward. One of the earlier of these forms is that of the boy Heru standing on crocodiles, and grasping scorpions and poisonous animals in his hands.

Amon was the local god of Karnak, and owed his importance in Egypt to the political rise of his district later. His name means 'that which is hidden'. He is the principle of creation within the darkness of chaos.

Mut, the great mother, was the goddess of Thebes. Later she became the wife of Amon. Her name means 'mother' and she leads and protects the kings, and the queens. The Vulture, who was a good role model of parenting, was Mut's totem. She is what many neo-pagans come to associate with the Goddess. All of creation was born within her womb.

Khonsu was the god of time (mostly because the moon regulated of the calendar). He was a moon god and his name means 'traveller'. He was a messenger of the Gods and was a child in the morning and an old man in the evening. (As was Re) As the New Moon he helped the land to become fruitful and women to conceive.

Anit (Neith) may have come from Libya. She was a goddess of hunting and of weaving, the two arts of a nomadic people. Her emblem was a staff with two crossed arrows. Her name comes from Netet which means 'to weave' and this made Neit as the weaver of the universe and destiny. In later times she was the watery mass from which the Sun emerged. How these different roles came about is unclear, but she must have merged with many other Gods and Goddesses, such as Mut, to get these attributes.

Re was the great sun god. During our period he was less important than Heru the Hawk sun god. Although Re existed in our period, he became more important during fourth dynasty. By the fifth dynasty a group called the called sons of Re proved themselves politically and later Pharaohs had the title "son of Re" before their name.

Atmu was the original god of Heliopolis and the Delta side, round to the gulf of Suez, which formerly reached up to Ismailiyeh. He was the setting sun and became linked with Re at a later period. He is an important figure to the Egyptian shaman because it is through his help the souls of the dead got into paradise. He was the first god depicted as a human.

Nut, is embodies heaven. Her name means 'night' and she is a female figure dotted over with stars. No temples have been found to her, nor was she associated with any particular place. She was more of a cosmogonist's idea. Nut bends over the earth, in all art representing her. Unseen, because of the two-dimensional nature of Egyptian art, is that her limbs are spread to the four quarters. She was a cosmic mother and a consort to Geb. Geb, was the earth god, who lay on the ground while Nut bends over him. He was the "prince of the gods," the power that went before all the later gods, the superseded Saturn of Egyptian theology. Like his consort Nut, so far no temples have been found dedicated to him, but he appears in the cosmic mythology. It seems, from their positions, that possibly the Set and Nut were the primeval gods before the Ausar worshippers of European type ever entered the Nile Valley.

Shu was the god of space, who lifted Nut from off the body of Seb. His image was everywhere, especially in late amulets. Believers hoped he would raise up their dead bodies earth to heaven. His figure is human, and he kneels on one knee with both hands lifted above his head. He was the father of Geb, the earth having been formed from space or chaos. His emblem was the ostrich feather because it is light and yet large.

Hapi, was one of the Gods of the Nile. He had a human form with large female breasts to show that he was the nourisher of the valley. More than 100 Shrines sacred to him were dotted along the Nile.

Ptah, the creator god, was worshipped at. Memphis. He is likely to have been a bit later than our period because he is drawn as an archetypal mummy. Recent archaeology has found that this form of mummification started during the first dynasty, but not in pre-dynastic times. Ptah could have been a god of pottery as he creates by modelling clay.

Amsu was depicted as a man with an erect penis. Worshipped mainly at Ekhmim and Koptos, he was the god of the desert, fertility and male sexuality. He is shown as standing above water, which suggests the fertility of the Nile. One of the oldest statues of any of the gods are three limestone figures of Amsu found at Koptos. These have relief designs of Red Sea shells and swordfish.

Het-hor was the female principle whose animal was the cow. Most of her roles were later taken by the mother Aset, but she managed to preserve her identity until the end of Egyptian religion. During our period she was popular. Her name means House of Heru, in other words she was the house in which the Hawk god lived. This house was a part of the watery mass that was heaven (although later Het-hor came to represent the whole sky). Later she became the great

Cosmic Mother.

Set: Set was later considered as the Egyptian Satan, however during our period that role was played by Apep. Some think his name means "stone", others say "cut" or "tail". However during our period he was as good as any other of the Gods and was worshipped in the South and Nubia and Libyan desert. His energy was supposed to help the dead climb the ladder to heaven. He was a God of the desert (as desert animals were sacrificed to him), of power and perhaps the night's sky. In later times he is seen as working against the flow of Order and his battles with Heru might a fight between night and day.

These gods lived like humanity. They could die, they could get old, sick and injured. One myth tells how Re, bitten by a magic serpent, suffers extreme pain. The Gods and Goddesses needed offerings of food and drink and had harems of concubines. Unless someone tells them, the Gods didn't know what was going on in earth and needed to send messengers. The only difference between them and mortals was they lived longer and had greater specialised powers.

When an Egyptian wanted to secure a god's favour they would make an offering and simply ask for help.

During the pre-dynastic and early dynastic periods there was less polytheism than we see during later periods. Most people would worship only one or two gods for their area. As regions linked, more gods became available to each village. Finally as the country became unified under various Pharaohs, a more polytheistic approach is developed. The increasing priesthoods started to classify the various gods into families and link them into legends. According to Budge over the centuries the number of Gods and Goddesses started to shrink. In Gods of the Egyptians he says:

> *"This reduction in the number of Gods began when man realised that some were mightier than others, for he had ceased gradually to worship those who had, in his opinion, failed to justify his belief in them, and transferred his allegiance to those Gods who were able to give him the most help. In the process of time the god or goddess of a certain village or town would obtain fame and reputation for*

power which would out-rival those deities of neighbouring cities and a growth of the worship of such God and Goddesses would be accompanied by a corresponding decline in that of the Gods in the towns around."

In the beginning...

The Ancient Egyptians had several creation myths with varying degrees of complexity. These myths had an elaborate philosophy that has something in common with modern quantum physics. Put simple everything in the universe, nature and life came from Chaos. The word they used for Chaos was 'Isfet' which and the universe, or order (Maat), was its opposite.

According to the Pyramid texts, which are most ancient religious texts we have, the Egyptians believed that Chaos was a period where everything only existed in potential. It was like a random ocean of possibilities from which order sprang. However this is a puzzle. How can Order appear from Chaos? There is a clue in Pyramid text 1466 which describes a Pharaoh as 'being fashioned' by Atum before the sky, earth, men, gods and even death existed. In other words within the folds of chaos there is an urge to create and the will to bring order.

One of the translations of Atum's name could be "total", this implies a supreme and unalterable state of perfection that emerges from chaos. Everything was part of Atum. This is an important principle which counters those who would have the Egyptians as a dualist or pantheistic religion. If everything emerges from the creative will of a single being, then it means there is a tendency towards monotheism throughout Egypt's history, at least among the intellectual and religious elite.

The Nile was the inspiration for their approach to the Universe. Imagine that you saw the Nile as it flooded. The whole area would be swamped by rushing dirty random water. After a while, as if by a signal by an unseen force, the waters would retreat and reveal fertile black earth. From this earth trees and plants would grow.

Atum, rises from the waters of chaos and, while sitting alone on the primeval mound that rose above chaos, he masturbated (created from himself). Shu and Tefnut were born from this act and from this god and goddess the rest of the universe was built.

This act of creation, which was re-enacted in the Temple of Karnak every day for nearly three thousand years reflects a lot about what the Egyptians thought about life. To them everything was cyclic. The sun was born in the East, set in the west, died at midnight, and found life in the darkness. There was an order to such an existence, Maat (who was a goddess of Truth) made sure that everything lasted for millions of years.

Egyptians feared chaos, which was present in their universe and could destroy the Natural order. Chaos's curse extended not only to the physical realm, but could destroy all the Gods too. Atum admits that one day he will drown gods, men and the Earth in the primal chaotic waters and only he and Ausar will survive. This perhaps hints that only the best in human potential (Ausar) will survive the end of the universe.

According to the Egyptians, the earth had been created by the word of a God. The Egyptians believed that by naming something you could cause and object to exist. In fact they even had a God who was supposed to represent the power of the divine word - Hu.

He personifies the authority of utterance. He was the partner of Sia who personified Divine Knowledge. With the falcon-headed Sun God, Re they rode the Sun boat across the sky to create and continue all life. This idea becomes important later when we look at the Egyptian uses of magic.

Another important creation myth, which has elements of an earlier shamanic tale was the sun was an egg laid by a primeval goose.

The Egyptians believed the world was flat. Over it the sun passed during the day and went beneath it at night. Immediately above the earth is the air, which was held up by four pillars and above that was a vault of water. The sun floated on this heavenly ocean.

It is important to understand the Egyptians were insular; the world ended at the borders of Egypt. This must have taken a great deal mental juggling as the Egyptians had much contact with outsiders.

Egypt was invaded, settled by, and traded with foreign cultures and yet the population remained philosophically distant from the rest of the world. This has parallels with Ancient and Medieval China and Japan, who despite being aware of other cultures preferred not to think about them.

Mummies, Ausar and life after death

During the later pre-dynastic period, the way the living and the dead interacted was changed by the idea of the Kingdom of Ausar.

We will look at Ausar in detail later in this book. He is the God of the Dead above all others. When you died you were brought before him for judgment. If you were declared to be a balanced and good individual you could live in Ausar's kingdom.

Originally this kingdom had a physical position in the marshlands of the Delta, however later as too many 'living' people lived there it was transferred to Syria. Finally Ausar's Kingdom was declared to be in the Northeast of the sky, where the Milky Way became the heavenly Nile.

Until the Egyptians came in touch with the Greeks, the Kingdom of Ausar was a mirror of Earth where the main occupation in this kingdom was agriculture. Souls ploughed the land, sowed the corn, and reaped the harvest of maize. They rowed and played the sports. They ate bread-cakes, drank beer had sex and had the company of their relations and friends. Each comfort was achieved by using magical words of power.

The Ancient Egyptians believed the dead needed feeding. They believed that part of the person went to the Kingdom of Ausar, but another part of the spirit would return to the tomb and wanted food. They would visit the graves of their ancestors and leave offerings.

During the first dynasty the rich would be preserved and wrapped in bandages. By the third and fourth dynasties Priests of Anu cut the body open and removed its perishable organs. A natural drying agent: natron, a salt-like substance which was found in a desert valley west of the Delta today called "Natron Valley" (Wadi el Natrun) was used as a preservative. Amulets magically preserving the body appear during this time, although the full development of the amulet was in the twenty-sixth to thirtieth dynasties.

Packs of linen were stuffed into the body cavity to restore its shape. Wide strips of linen soaked in an adhesive, were wound around the body. After the adhesive had set, a thin layer of plaster, painted to resemble the deceased. It was not until the Middle Kingdom they used "true" mummification the form most of us understand it.

But there was no particular reverence given to the dead body and Egyptologists can't explain why they took such efforts to preserve the body with mummification. Some believe the reason was to prevent them coming to life again. The logic (and I use the term loosely) is that many primitive societies have a fear of roaming dead spirits attacking them. Since these spirits were released when the body collapsed keeping them preserved forced them to stay in the tomb.

However there is a magical reason for preservation of the body. The mummy was a talisman acting as a sympathetic link between the various parts of the soul. Keeping the body preserved for as long as possible would make it a powerful symbol of the immortality.

After preparing the dead, the funeral rites began. The body was lain out in its coffin on a couch and mourning took place. Then there was a procession to carry the body to its tomb, often by a boat. At the tomb, various specific ceremonies were performed, including the ritual of the "Opening of the Mouth". The ritual needed more than one hundred actions by a Sem priest. He would symbolically break open the mouth of the body or of a statue of the deceased with two tools. The first, the Pesh en Kef, was a two-bladed tool and there was an Adze so the spirits of the dead could return to the body or the statue.

In later, more elaborate tombs, they placed the coffin in a sarcophagus in the tomb's burial chamber. Before sealing the tomb grave offerings were carried into the burial chamber. Back at the deceased person's home, the funeral finished with an elaborate funeral wake.

The Time of the Shaman

The development of Nomes

During the Gerzean period the villages had grown into towns which were the centre of regions, or hespu. The Greeks called these regions Nomes, which is the title we are stuck with. We do not know when this division of the country happened, but it was early in Egypt's history. Nor do we know how many Nomes there were, some Egyptian sources say 42 others 44.

This regionalisation shows a growing sense of identity of the Nile based communities. No longer did they see themselves as living in a particular village, but as part of a greater whole.

Archaeology has revealed these Nomes were nothing more than petty kingdoms often fighting with its neighbours. It shows significant economic growth caused in part by trade. Goods from Nubia, Libya and the thriving economies of Mesopotamia have been found in Egypt.

Besides the Nomes there were two clear and sophisticated regions identified by the titles Upper and Lower Egypt.

Each region had two 'capitals' in the North there was Dep and Pe (collectively called Buto) while in the south there were Nekhen and Nekheb. It is likely the se were just four Kingdoms that were more powerful and united other Nomes in the region. Of Dep and Pe there is little known other than the fact they worshipped Wadjet, who was a female cobra and a heron (whose name is lost). In Nekhen was worshipped a male hawk and in Nejhbet a vulture.

But with this regionalisation there was an idea forming which would be developed during the Dynastic period.

We start to see the animal totems becoming regionalised. On the many pots found during the pre-dynastic period artists have depicted animal and god standards being carried on boats. These are shorthand for where the boat came from. An elephant standard is carried on boats that came from the Elephantine, two crossed arrows to represent Neith from Sais.

On both Scorpion and Narmer's mace-heads we can see their attendants carrying standards which bear the totemic animals of the various Nomes that were loyal to them. Scorpion has griffin-like creatures to represent the Nomes he has conquered.

One motif repeated on many jars is of a many-oared ship. Aboard is a large figure of a woman with her hands raised in a ritualistic gesture. Attending her are one sometimes two smaller male figures and there are sometimes animals aboard these ships. No crew are visible.

The Nomes were an integral part of the Egyptians' idea of themselves and their country. In Dynastic times the standards from each Nome were a part of a key ritual called the Heb-Sed. This ceremony was the method the Pharoah symbolically renewed his sovereignty and rule of the country.

Scenes on the walls of a Dendra temple show a delegation of priests arriving for a council in which each priest carried a standard bearing the Nome of the city he represented. It is possible the Nome standards could have stood in the boundaries of their provinces, much as road signs do today.

In his book 'Early Hydraulic Civilisation in Egypt; a study in cultural ecology'[3] , Karl Butzer suggests the Nomes could have had socioeconomic and ecological implications. The Nome may have been a way of marking out irrigation networks, which became the basis of settled village life. Effective management of the land was the job of the Pharoah and some of the early rulers are depicted digging canals.

The Nomes are important to an understanding of the way Egypt mapped out their spiritual landscape. The Egyptians believed their country was a mirror of both heaven and the Underworld. Each Nome had a God or Goddess appointed to rule it and was given a heavenly and underworld location. Just as you could journey on a boat up the Nile, it was possible to sail on the Heavenly Nile, which was the Milky Way, or through the river of the Underworld through the various Cities of the Dead.

There is an idea the Nomes had a physical correspondence on the human body and therefore a god or goddess in charge. This has

---

[3] Early Hydrologic Civilisation in Egypt; A study in cultural ecology, Karl Butzer, University of Chicago Press, Chicago, 1976.

important for a shaman who is seeking to heal a person by appealing to the god in charge of that part of the body.

Unfortunately the names we have for the Nomes come from a much later period of Egyptian history. Some of the names of the some of the animal totems have disappeared but those that do, such as mountain bull, ibis, fish and the oryx, give us a clear idea of how this worked.

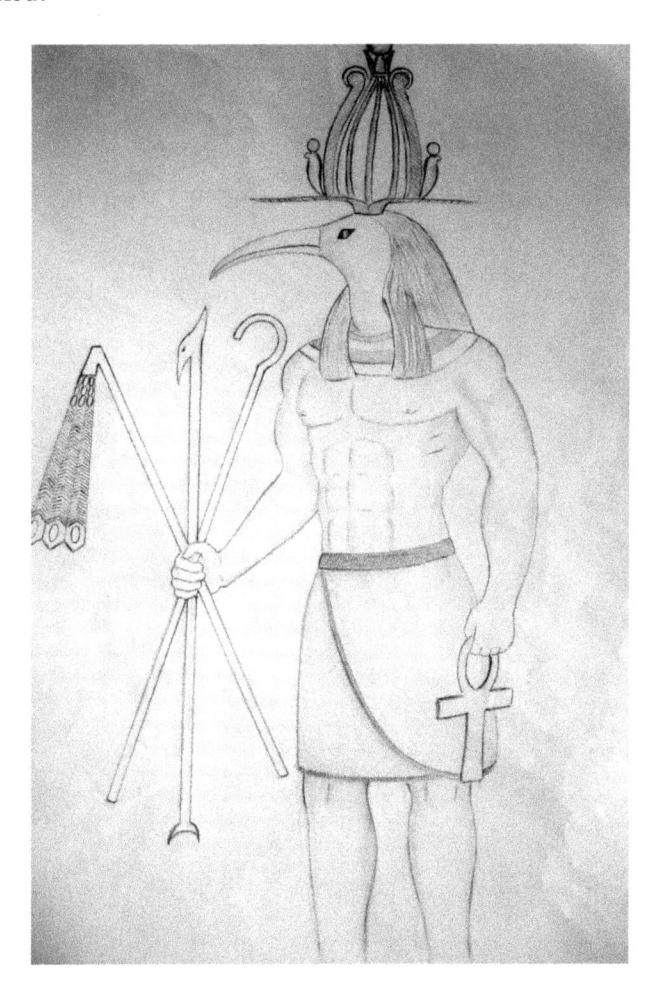

THOTH
ILLUSTRATION BY PAOLA FARRELL

Egyptian Nome Names of Upper and Lower Egypt

Upper Egypt

1. Ta-Sety
2. Throne of Heru
3. Shrine
4. Sceptre
5. Two Falcons
6. Crocodile
7. Sistrum
8. Great Land
9. Amsu
10. Cobra
11. Set

12. Viper
13. Upper Sycamore
14. Lower Sycamore
15. Hare
16. Oryx
17. Jackel
18. Anti
19. Two Sceptres
20. South Sycamore
21. Northern Sycamore
22. Knife

Lower Egypt

1. White Wall
2. Foreleg
3. West
4. Southern Shield
5. Northern Shield
6. Mountain Bull
7. Western Harpoon
8. Eastern Harpoon
9. Andjety
10. Black Ox
11. Ox-Count
12. Calf and Cow
13. Prospering Sceptre
14. Foremost of the East
15. Ibis
16. Fish
17. Behdet
18. Prince of the South
19. Prince of the North
20. Plumed Falcon

The Gods of the Nomes during the Dynastic Period

Nome	Capital	God
Upper Egypt		
1. Ta-Khent	Abu	Khnemu
2. Thes Hertu	Teb	Heru-Behutet
3. Ten	Nekeb	Nekhebet
4. Uast	Uast	Amon-Re
5. Herui	Qebti	Amsu
6. Aa-Ta	Ta-en-tarert	Het-hor
7. Seshesh	Het	Het-hor
8. Abt	Abtu and This	An-Her
9. Amsu	Apu	Amsu
10. Uatchet	Tebut	Het-hor
10a Neterui	Tu-qat	Heru
11. Set	Shas-hetep	Khnemu
12. Tu-F	Nut-end-bak	Heru
13. Atef-Khent	Saiut	Ap-uat
14. Atef-Pehu	Qesi	Het-hor
15. Un	Khemennu	Tehuti
16. Meh Mahetch	Hebennu	Heru
17. Anpu	Kasa	An-pu
18. Sep	Het-suten	An-pu
19. Uab	Per Matchet	Set
20. Atef-Khent	Henensu	Her-shefi
21. Atef-Pehu	Ermen-Hert	Khnemu
21a Ta-She	Shet	Sebek
22. Maten	Tep-ahet	Het-hor
Lower Egypt		
1. Aneb Hetch	Men-nefert	Ptah
2. Kensu	Sekhemt	Heru-ur
3. Ament	Nut-ent-Hap	Apis

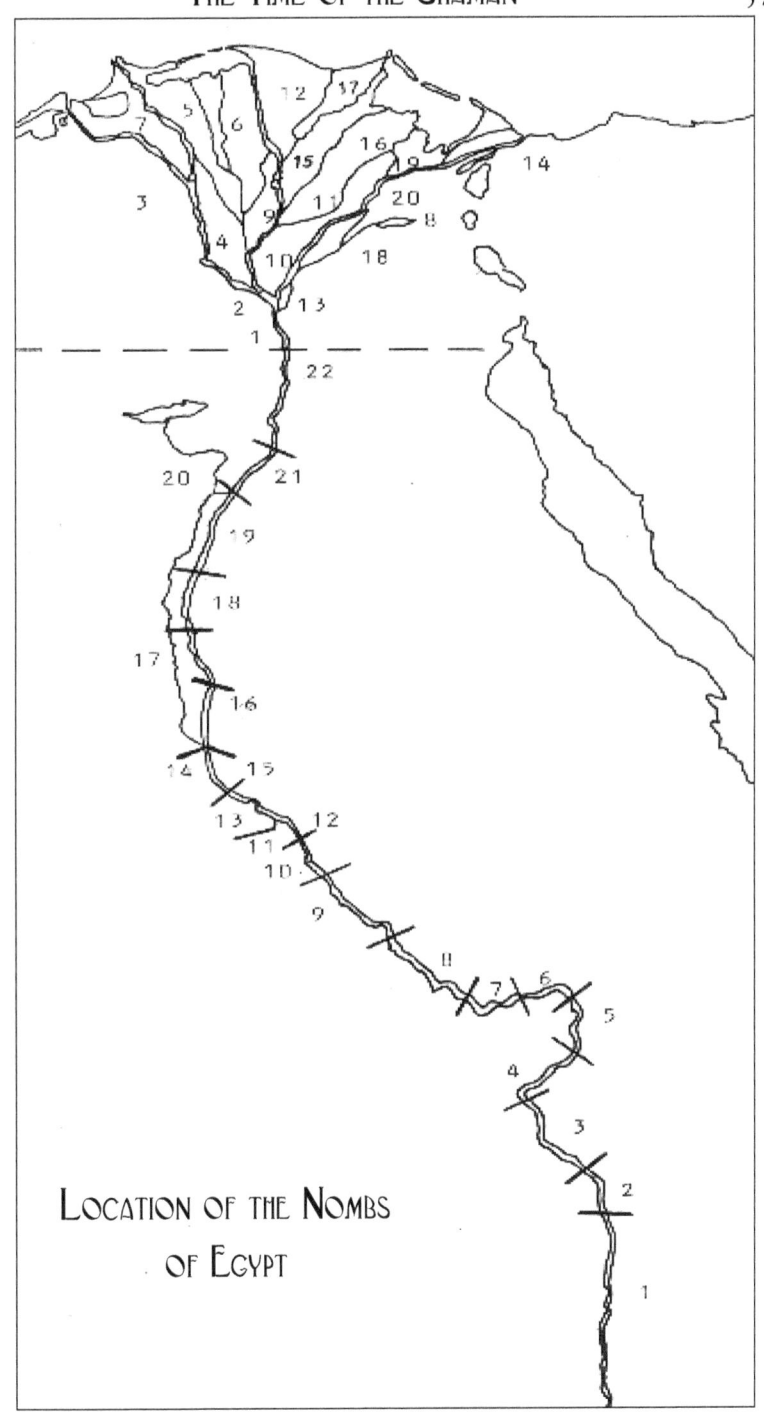

The Time of the Shaman

Location of the Nombs of Egypt

4. Sapi-Res	Tcheqa	Sebek
5. Sap-Meh	Saut	Neith
6. Kaset	Khasut	Amon-Re
7. Ament	Senti nefert	Hu
8. Abt	Theket	Temu
9. Ati	Per Asar	Ausar
10. Ka-Qem	Het-ta-her-ab	Heru
11. Ka-Heseb	Hebese-Ka	Aset
12. Theb-ka	Theb-neter	An-Her
13. Heq At	Annu	Re
14. Khent-Abt	Tchalu	Heru
15. Tehut	Per-Tehuti	Tehuti
16. Kha	Per-ba-neb Tettu	Ba-neb-Tattu
17. Sam Behutet	Pa-khen-en-Amon	Amon-Re
18. Am Khent	Per-Bastet	Bastet
19. Am-Pehu	Per Uatchet	Uatchet
20. Sept	Qesem	Sept

The Time of the Shaman

The Shaman in the Midst

The Sem Priest
Illustration by Billy Walker~John

Magic was a key part of humanity's relationship with the Gods. Reciting the right prayer, hymn or designing a talisman was the job of the village specialist. This was a shamanic figure who was responsible for representing his village in discussions with the Gods and Goddesses and the Spirits of the Ancestors.

The Shaman would probably have the job of exorcising and

appeasing the various Gods and Goddesses, healing villagers and scaring off the bad forces that effected the area and crops. It is likely the people considered their chief a God – either as a representative of a deity on earth or as a collective soul of the village.

Throughout this period the Egyptian shaman had evolved with his or her country. They would have started out as the representative of the Gods and spiritual adviser to the village heads. He or she would not have been called a shaman, of course. That was a title given to those spiritual tribal leaders who ruled in the frozen Siberian wastes. Nor would the patronising label of witch doctor be fitting either. That label comes from a Christian belief the pagan tribes that Europeans met with were practicing back magic. Indeed we are uncertain precisely what the pre-dynastic Egyptians called their spiritual leaders.

One good candidate is the old title of Sem, which we mentioned earlier. We know that in New Kingdom times a priest called Kha'muast, the fourth son of the famous Rameses II, revived the title'.

Before the fourth dynasty it was a title given to the royal sons. Later when the priesthood was considered an important place for royal training the title became clearly associated with the Priesthood. However when you believed that your royalty were Gods, as the ancient and pre-dynastic Egyptians did, the distinction becomes blurred. A Pharaoh's son was the God Heru and the communicator of his father's will on earth after the latter's death.

In the religious texts that have come down to us the Sem Priest is depicted performing a ritual called Opening the Mouth which allows a statue or dead person to speak. During a funeral ritual the entranced Sem Priest would be dragged on a sled covered in a blanket. As the rite progressed the Sem Priest would reveal first his head, then his body and finally would emerge from his trance to open the mouth of the dead person with a special iron tool.

The Sem priest is depicted as wearing an animal skin, usually a leopard, although some sources say a panther. The leopard had a strong association with the lands of the dead and by wearing its skin, it is likely the Sem believed they had its powers in these realms. They have their hair plated in a lock over the right side the head, much like the youthful depiction of the God Heru.

His role is clearly what many would recognise as shamanic. He enters a trance and acts as a voice between living and the dead and giving both a voice each other's realms.

There is a scenario by which the Sem could have changed from village shaman in pre-dynastic times to the Pharaoh's priestly son of later periods. As the villages got bigger the shaman's role would have become more important. Eventually, it would be politically expedient for a village ruler to give it to his most trusted adviser.

While a priesthood could be trusted to take care of the rituals associated with the Gods or totem animals. But the shaman who mediated messages from beings from the lands of the dead or the Gods was a more important character. If you were a ruler you would not want your shaman to give politically off-message material. Eventually the only person who could be trusted would be a relative who has an investment in your rulership – your son.

We are looking at a period where rulers were equated to gods, so it is natural their offspring would be the best people to walk between the worlds, until they became gods too. By the end of the archaic period the Sem Priests were the sons of the ruler and the Egyptian shamans had a role they would keep until Christianity was adopted in Egypt during the time of Constantine.

I should point out there is little historical proof of this other than the shamanic responsibilities of the Sem Priests of later periods. However I am not the first to make the link. In their book 'Inner Guide to Egypt' Alan Richardson and Billy Walker-John say:

> "The Sem, as the focus for the consciousness of the people as a whole worked changes within his own psyche and the psyches of his followers. This was the true purpose of the Sem. In previous ages it was the role of the Shaman. Despite the complexity of worship in Egypt and the extraordinarily developed theocracies, striking parallels with shamanism in its pure and simple form wherein a man or a woman would act as a link between the tribe, its ancestors

and animal spirits and the area in which they lived."

Walker-John and Richardson make a link between the Sem's quenau (skin cloak) which is called the coat of protection which parallels the ritual clothing worn by a shaman in any other cultures would wear on his journey to the otherworld.

This argument has been noticed in the more orthodox world of Egyptologists. W Helk[4] suggests the Sem priest, whose leopard skin cloak shows parallels with the shaman chiefs of some recent African societies, is evidence that shamanism may have been practised at least in early Dynastic times .

Cloaks were worn in Egyptian art by the dead and by kings during certain festivals. Until the Middle Kingdom coffins were draped in a leopard skin, perhaps suggesting a belief the dead was on a shamanic outing.

Helk sees the ritual of opening the mouth which had to be conducted by a Sem priest as further proof of the way shamans entered Dynastic Egypt.

Greg Reeder[5] in his article on the mysterious tekenu figure depicted on in different stages that puzzled Egyptologists on many dynastic tombs was the Sem priest in seen during various parts of Opening the Mouth ritual . First, the entranced Sem would be wrapped in a blanket and dragged on a sled to the ritual. Next he is seen with his head poking out of the blanket, then in a fetal position and finally standing offering incense during the Opening of the Mouth ritual.

As well as the role of dealing with the dead an Egyptian Shaman would have been responsible for performing magical acts for his community. The populace did not believe they had the skill, education to approach the God themselves and succeed. So they outsourced the task to their priesthood or village shaman.

The priest or shaman would perform ceremonious, sacrifices, prayers, and chants, which the god himself had taught him. The pre-dynastic Egyptian thought that if he built a fetish either in the

---

[4] Helk, W., 1984. 'Schamane und Zauberer' in M'langes Adolphe Gutbub. Montpellier University, Paul Vatery de Montpelier. pp103-108.
[5] Greg Reeder, KMT: A Modern Journal of Ancient Egypt, Fall, 1994, Vol 5, No 3

human shape or in that of an animal, by threats or coaxing, he could make it come alive with a spiritual force.

In Egyptian magic it was normal to force the gods into doing his bidding. In the Pyramid Texts, the deceased Pharaoh is said to threaten to eat the Gods if they do not open the Gates of the Sky. This is rare in religion as most gods are supposed to be so powerful they cannot become any mortal's tool. This has much in common with Hinduism where even the most powerful of gods are compelled by the practice of "Fierce Asceticism".

Chapter Two

Shamans ~ Ancient and Modern

During the last thirty years we have seen a rebirth of spiritual techniques that more shamanistic. Drawing on many cultural sources, mainly Native American Indian, modern neo-pagans have created a system boiled down to several techniques and spiced with the various traditions that have taken their fancy. Although the techniques may be similar to Lakota, Maori, or the Siberian Shaman it is so shaped by Anglo-European culture that it has become a different animal.

This is not bad. By applying, what many call core shamanistic techniques it is possible to take the symbolism the practitioner responds to best with and forge a spiritual song built from many symbolic notes. These culturally patchwork shamans can explore the inner realities of view point of countless different myths.

When we are looking to build a shamanic system based on the symbolism of Ancient Egypt we most first look at some of the modern core techniques. Then we need to work out which ones are right for Ancient Egypt and see what needs to be rejected or added.

One definition of a modern shaman is someone who changes their consciousness to experience another reality to bring healing to themselves and their environment. By 'healing', I mean it in its widest spiritual sense. I would define a person who makes a connection with their higher spiritual self, what we call our Holy Guardian Angel in the Hermetic tradition as being 'healed'.

The core techniques of shamanism are:

1. The purification and consecration of the priest and space.
2. Healing
3. The use of trance, chant, drum, dance, or ceremony to achieve a raised state of consciousness.
4. The visiting of different inner locations during in dream and trance.
5. Communication and alliances with Spirits – whether these be animal, ancestors, or divine beings.
6. Shapeshifting, that is moving into different forms to understand the nature of reality from its perspective.
7. Worship of unity through diversity

These core techniques differ slightly from other paths of spirituality. First shamans do not regard themselves as a priest, although in some traditional societies they held that role. It is not his or her job to lead the congregation towards divinity but rather build a bridge between the spirits and reality.

Shamanism is a direct spiritual experience. It is not a system of faith; it is one of experience based on all senses. It is not a religion. Its techniques can be, and are, practised within existing religion. My greatest shamanic teachers have been a pentecostal missionary, a liberal catholic priest, a Hasidic Jew and a Bulgarian Orthodox homemaker. They might have been seen as holding 'unusual religious views' by their respective faiths, but they took their religion seriously.

There are many who see Egyptian magic either as an intellectual or internal path. The pre-dynastic shaman would not have seen it that way. Their s is an internal and an external path. There is trance work, but there is an important element of doing things in nature too. Many meditators and intellectuals in the Western Esoteric Tradition say they are dedicated to finding God in Nature. However if they are not keen in leaving their houses, flats, or meditation rooms they will never have this experience.

You cannot understand Re if your do not feel his power beating down on you at noon in midsummer. You cannot understand the symbolism of his fight with Apep, if you have not seen the sun rise among blood coloured clouds of morning. Sure, you might have seen this on television, but the real shaman wants to see it and experience it.

Shamanism does not use abstract symbols that stimulate the intellect. To the shaman that which is found on the earth has a direct link with the underworld or spiritual realm. There is no need to have a cross to explain the four elements of fire, water, earth and air when you have the real thing all around you.

All these things make shamanism the white-water rafting of spiritual paths. It is the greatest of uncontrolled fun, but it is one of the most dangerous and hardest. Unlike Wicca, or ceremonial magic, the shaman does not have the luxury of a system that works like a trellis to encourage early growth. As in the many forms of mysticism, what you learn about the universe as a Shaman flows like a river. Often it goes back on itself. You might learn about Nature one week you reverse the next. In the end, only the path is the real teacher.

Spirits, particularly those at a lower level, can be troublesome to both property and the shaman's mental state. You cannot turn off the tap once you have started. The spirits cry out from every rock and tree and you feel the pain of your community more acutely.

So, it is not surprising that when a Siberian community identified a prospective shaman, that person would often run off out of fear. One elderly friend of mine said that it was only that her own internal spirit that kept her from quitting and forgetting all about shamanism.

The modern Shaman when using the symbolism of pre-dynastic Egypt has to remember this. They have to remember that we are approaching a system that is thousands of years old. The pre-dynastic shaman, who visited the underworld, did not have an idea of medicine, computers, electricity, or television. Some Egyptians may have been aware of people in far-off lands, but most never left their village (let alone their Nome). When we use Egyptian formula, we are closer to a more primitive part of ourselves. Most of our primitive traits are kept under psychic lock and key and tamed with a steady diet of soap operas and computer games.

Yet the symbolism of pre-dynastic Egypt will answer a cry from deep within us if we let it and will serve to balance the demands that modern society has thrown on us.

Preparing the Ground

Before beginning on the path of an Egyptian Shaman, it is important to prepare yourself to handle the spiritual symbols that will become your regular way of life. In this book, I have assumed that a person is living in an urban environment. I have done this mostly because it is the 'worst case scenario' as far as approaching nature is concerned. These exercises are designed to counter your urban environment and allow you to find peace in the middle of it. You will have to be prepared to get away from it all and into nature occasionally for important ceremonies.

Relaxing

A shaman needs is to achieve a deep state of relaxation at will. Relaxation is the way the body consciousness is disabled and the more relaxed you can be the more 'real' the next world will be. A shaman, of course, needs to get to an altered state that is more than mere relaxation, it is a deep state called a trance. Achieving a usable trance state takes time and you will need to first shed the cares of your life and focus within.

Basic Relaxation technique

Sit in a straight-backed chair with your hands on your thighs. When you are comfortable, regulate your breathing. Breathe in and out as slowly and as deeply as you can. Say you yourself, as I breathe out all tension is leaving my body and as I breathe in, I shall relax further.

Now think of each part of your body, one by one, starting with your feet. Say to yourself, as I breathe out any tenseness in my feet will leave and as I breath in my feet shall relax. Do this until that part of the body is relaxed. Gradually move up your body, tensing and relaxing each muscle. Do not forget to relax the face and back of the head. There will be some parts of the body that will be tenser than others and will want special attention. If you wear glasses you might find the muscles around your eyes will take more effort you pay to it the greater the rewards.

When you have completed your relaxation (and this can take 15 minutes to half an hour for the first few times) say to yourself "I will now become more deeply relaxed".

Try this exercise several times. Allow yourself to daydream. Just let your mind wander. After a while allow yourself to 'wake up' slowly move your body and note down your experiences. This will be your first experience of trance work.

Trance

A trance is a gradually deepening from of altered state of consciousness. The shaman will use many different ways to get into a trance including drugs, drumming, chanting, breathing and dancing and we will look at some of these later. If you can archive such a state (even if it is only lightly) naturally you will be more susceptible to such techniques later. Instead of being dependent on the drum or chant, you can use them to send you deeper.

The goal of the trance is to open your consciousness enough to hallucinate. The word hallucinate carries with it ideas of illusion, but in fact it means to experience something with your senses that another objective person would not. There are different levels of trance and many of them you would not see as any different from your normal state.

There are 11 levels of consciousness and it is worthwhile to compare these levels with the notes you made of your relaxation work.

1. Being awake and fully aware of your surroundings. This needs practice as few people experience their surroundings. The work of the shaman is to bring awareness of the other realms into this level of consciousness.

2. A daydream. The person is aware of their surroundings and able to write, keyboard, mix paints, and even drive a car and interact with the world around them.

3. Absorption in a subject so deep that if someone speaks to them they are slow to respond. They may answer questions and without being fully aware of it.

4. Concentrated away from the material world. A person is open to seeing the interrelatedness of all and less likely to self-censor that information.

5. A deep absorption in the mind and the imagination. A person is able to shift awareness from the trance and into the material world without difficulty, although there is often disorientation after a sudden transition. The journey state where a person is focused on their imaginary world and works in a linear fashion. This a pathworking trance (see my book *Magical Pathworking*).

6. The shaman intentionally removes her awareness from the material world and enters the Otherworld. The shaman is less aware of his physical body than level 5 trance. It seems remote. This sometimes happens during a pathworking when a person jumps out of the plot and the imagery becomes less rational. The journey becomes less linear and more dreamlike. Shamans in this stage of trance cannot easily manage their bodies and are usually sitting or lying down.

7. The shaman has the same level of their body as they have when they are sleeping. They are awake and acting in another world. They see this other realm as a reality. The person will meet otherworld entities and not have control over the answers. Most of the senses are used including a sense of touch.

8. This is the deepest stage of shamanic trance. It is similar to level seven except all the laws of reality take a break. It is possible move through landscapes or creates our own landscapes. We may assume complete control of where we go and what we do, just as we assume control of our waking actions. Physical senses are disabled; or rather we are sensing objects with spiritual senses. This gives us a total vision and sound. Communication appears chaotic in that it is not linear. A being might say something to you in an instant that if you

were to write down would fill several books. Some people report experiences they can hear colours and see sounds. This is similar to early LSD experiences and the reports of those who have experimented with 'magic mushrooms' of the South American traditions.

9. The individually is merged with the vision. The sense of identity which has permeated the previous stages has slipped away and been replaced by new consciousness. There is a sense of total unity, but at the same time a sense of being connected with it. This is one of the highest states of consciousness reported by mystics. There is a sense of being "one with the Father".

10. This point is beyond spiritual vision, or indeed description. In the East it is described as the state of complete enlightenment.

In their book, *The Shamans of Prehistory: Trance and Magic in the Painted Caves*[1], Jean Clottes and David Lewis-Williams report their experiments with people in altered states. More scientifically based, they assign only three levels of trance defined by what the people see. In the first stage, people "see" brightly coloured geometric forms, such as dots, zigzags, grids, sets of parallel lines, nested curves, and meandering lines. These are similar to the rock engravings (petroglyphs) of the southern African plateau. Indeed the writers said that when the eyes of the person in a light trance were opened they could be projected onto walls. Some shamans would interpret these shapes by myth or legend.

During the second level of trance, these shapes become solid objects of religious or emotional significance. Round shapes might become cups and the shimmering zigzags might become a snake.

The third stage is reached after the subject is drawn into some vortex, or tunnel. Subjects feel themselves drawn into the vortex, at the end of which is a bright light. This is similar to what people describe during a near death experience, and there are some likenesses between someone in a deep trance and a corpse.

---

[1] *The Shamans of Prehistory: Trance and Magic in the Painted Caves*, by Jean Clottes and David Lewis-Williamspp

Shamans Ancient and Modern

When subjects come out of the tunnel or vortex, they find themselves seeing a different world. Monsters, people, and settings are intensely real.

The writers added that when a subject's eyes are open these hallucinations are projected onto the surrounding surfaces. Some reported that pictured floated before their imagination others said it was like watching a slide show. With eyes shut, it was easier for people to feel themselves as flying, changing into birds or animals.

"These three stages are universal and wired into the human nervous system, though the meanings given to the geometrics of Stage One, the objects into which they are illusioned in Stage Two, and the hallucinations of Stage Three are all culture-specific; at least in some measure, people hallucinate what they expect to hallucinate. A shaman may see an antelope; an Inuit will see a polar bear or seal. But, allowing for such cultural diversity, we can be sure the three stages of altered consciousness provide a framework for an understanding of shamanic experiences."

Postures

The idea of postures will be familiar to those who use Eastern techniques. In the East they are used to make sure the energy centres are aligned correctly to archive certain spiritual states.

In the Western Mystery tradition and shamanic traditions, postures are considered less important. In Egypt there are many different positions suggested on various tomb and papyrus. As a result, after we conducted a few experiments and found there was not only a physical practicality in some of them, but a symbolic one too. They improve the results of different types of meditation and trance work.

You should practice the different postures until you can relax at least as deeply as you did before. Some hurt when you first try them, however if you work gradually into them your joints will become more flexible.

You should practice holding these postures for as long as possible in a relaxed state. There is nothing wrong with sitting on a bed or cushion. Care must be taken with some of the lying down postures not to fall asleep.

The position of the scribe

This is sitting cross-legged with your back straight and your head looking directly ahead. This posture is a good general meditation, light trance, drumming and chant position.

The position of the kneeling supplicant

This is sitting on your heels. The hands are placed on the thighs and the back is kept straight. This posture is a good general meditation, light trance, drumming, worship and chant position.

The Sitting Shaman

The knees are bought up to the face and the arms are wrapped around the knees. This position calls for some balance. It is used for meditation and medium level trance.

The Birth and Death position

This is a fetal position. Traditionally you would lie on your left side, hands bought up to your face and knees up to your stomach. It is used for deep and medium level trance. Note that it can only be effective if you have not eaten or drunk for at least four hours, otherwise your growling stomach will distract you.

The Ausar Position

Lie flat on your back with your legs together. The right arm is laid over the left crossed over the chest. It is used for deep and medium level trance.

Compare your results with the relaxation exercise you did before.

What was different? Did some positions enable you to reach a deeper level? Why do you think that was? In my experience, some postures force me to become aware of my body and prevent me from reaching deeper states. Sometimes that is desirable. If I were doing a pathworking using set symbolism to understand a particular point, I would not want to enter higher than level five. Nothing brings me back faster than an awareness that my knees are hurting because I am sitting in the position of the kneeling supplicant.

Breathing

In Eastern techniques there are a battery of different breathing techniques designed to have different effects on the meditator. Altered breathing patterns build up subtle changes within the bloodstream and improve meditation and ritual work.

There is a practical reason to have control of your breath. In deep trance states, breathing will naturally slow down. If you cannot breathe naturally, you could be pulled out of a deep trance by your body demanding air. More than one person who uses shamanic techniques has found himself or herself waking up with a huge headache caused through a lack of oxygen during their trances.

Therefore, while there are fewer breathing techniques in the Western Mystery Tradition, the few we have are vital. The most common is called the fourfold breath and that will suit our purposes well initially. The fourfold breath is suitable for most pathworking and early purification work.

If practised often enough, so it becomes automatic, it will enable the shaman to breathe successfully through most trance states.

Fourfold Breath

You have to breathe from your diaphragm, which is below the rib cage in the abdomen. Do not speed up or force your breathing in anyway. It should be as natural as possible. It is unnecessary to pull in the breath or force anything, just push out the diaphragm, the rib cage will expand and air will rush into your lungs. Contracting the lungs will push out the old air -- you should not hear any sound or you are forcing the process too much, the solution is to slow down.

The process is to empty your lungs and then inhale deeply to a count of four. Hold the tightened diaphragm for a count of two; breathe out for a count of four; keep the tightened diaphragm for a count of two; then inhale to a count of four. The counting should be your own and matched to your own lung capacity.

Once you are relaxed this breath cycle should be fixed consciously for at least six full cycles.

Shamanic techniques involve chanting which regulates breath in its own way and to hit different states. We will look and this later.

The Sem Priest Blanket

Traditionally there is some form of magical blanket or cloak made from feathers, wool or animal skin that Shaman wraps themselves. It has several practical and spiritual uses. The first is obvious in that it keeps you warm when outdoors. This is important, when undergoing deep trance states where you lose body awareness and are unaware that you are cold. This could lead to hypothermia when you wake up. In some trances your body temperature drops and this aggravates the problem.

Another practical advantage, which anyone who has trouble waking up on a Monday morning will know, is that a blanket provides womb-like warmth. If you wrap yourself in a blanket and put your head under the covers, it is the closest state to returning to a mother's womb, where all the cares of the world are forgotten. This is the motivation behind a child keeping a 'security blanket' long after they have physically outgrown it.

To the Shaman the womb is a gateway between the worlds. It is where a soul dies to the spiritual realm and is born in the material level. To the pre-dynastic Egyptian Shaman, the grave held a similar role as it was the place where you transcended the physical world and entered the spiritual realm.

A womb has associations with protection and it is likely the blanket could have had this role; perhaps guarding the body while the shaman was journeying through the underworld. In an article for 'KMT: A Modern Journal of Ancient Egypt' Greg Reeder[2], pointed out the mysterious figure called a Tekenu shown taking part in the Opening of the Mouth Ritual was a Sem priest. In one 18th Dynasty tomb, the Sem is shown in the Tomb of Ramos wrapped in his blanket and in another of the same period he just has his head showing.

Although these tombs are much later than our period, the positioning is consistent with the use of the blanket by shamans in other cultures.

Although the Sem-Priest traditionally wears an animal skin, this would be too small to be wrapped around his body for trance work. Indeed, in the 18th Dynasty depiction, the Sem is wrapped in a striped blanket, which makes him look like a wasp.

With this historical background, clearly a modern shaman should have a blanket that which meets the following criteria:

1. It is large enough to sit on and cover the entire body and head.
2. It is warm enough.
3. It has a suitable pattern or colour.
4. It has some form of magical protection.

Proper patterns and colours would be blue with stars (to represent Nut), black, leopard spots, striped yellow and black or striped black and white. It could have an eye of Heru, or a hawk sewn onto it.

Weaving Protection into the Blanket

The blanket needs some form of ceremony to convert it from something mundane into something magical. To do this lay the blanket out flat so the corners face the compass points. You will need a fistful of salt (not sea salt) mixed with a teaspoon of bicarbonate of soda in a bowl, a bowl of water and a stick of incense. Put the bowl in the centre of the blanket. Sit cross-legged and pour the salt mixture into the water. Say four times:

---

[2] Greg Reeder, *KMT: A Modern Journal of Ancient Egypt*, Fall 1994, Vol 5, Number 3

"Natron purifies the waters of Nut"

Fling the water to the four quarters of the blanket and say four times to each quarter:

"This blanket is the Goddess and I am the son who is wrapped in the holy womb of her protection"

Wrap yourself in the blanket slowly and say four times:

"I am within the arms of Heru and he protects me. He closes his wings about me and I shall have no fear."

Allow yourself to go into a light trance. Picture the blanket becoming the wings of the might Hawk god. See them glow with golden power. Imagine him saying to you

"I am Heru. I have come that I might guard you. I have come that Nut may protect you, for she has embraced you. When you are in the embrace of Nut, there I am with you. "

When you are ready, allow your head to appear out of the blanket. Become aware of your surroundings and slowly unwrap yourself. Only use it for shamanic work and lock it away out of sight, perhaps in a special box.

The Egyptian body and soul

The Ancient Egyptians believed that a person was more than a physical body. Like much occult or New Age thought, they believed that a person comprised of different layers, which were like little beings. Initially it is likely the earliest Egyptians believed they had two bodies, a physical one and a shadow. After death, the body rotted and the shadow was free to haunt the underworld and the tomb.

However, a more elaborate structure for the body changed over time with more bodies added and some rejected. There were four main bodies, the physical one, the Ka, the Ba and the Ank.

The Ka is the spiritual powerhouse and causes the Body to work and move. The Ka gains this energy from food and drink. When you eat physical food, the Ka consumes its essence and converts it into something more useful. When are person is awake or alive, the Ka remains within the Body. It can and does leave the body when someone sleeps. The Ka is drawn back to the body by the need for food and protection. When the Body dies, the Ka separates from it, but must remain close. It still needs food and drink, or it will slowly crumble and slide into "nonexistence" or chaos.

Like the Ka, the Ba comes into existence at birth. Although some think that it is what the Egyptians considered the organ of thought (they thought the brain was responsible for giving you a runny nose), it is closer to what in modern psychology is called the Higher Self. It could fly between heaven and earth, returning to both the Ka and the Body to assure itself of their condition. After death, the Ba lived with the gods.

At death, another body called the Akh awakens. It is not certain if this lies dormant in the body during life and wakes up when a person dies or only exists after death. It separates from the body and this earth, never to return. One belief was that it rises to the boat of the sun and journeys with Re throughout eternity. More often, it moves off in search of the "Land of the Reeds", a heavenly version of the Nile Valley where it meets with the spirits of the ancestors and spends eternity among ever-fruitful fields and orchards.

To reach the "Land of the Reeds" the Akh faces gods and demons before arriving before Ausar for judgment. The person's life deeds were weighed on a balance-scale against Ma'at, the goddess of balance and order. If the Akh balanced the scales, the Akh joins Ausar in the Land of Reeds. The Akh is destroyed if it fails.

Besides these, there was the idea of a person's name as being essential part, almost a body in its own right. Ancient Egyptians believed that a person name must survive forever on earth in heaven and the netherworld. There were tablets outside some tombs that asked passersby to say the dead person's name aloud so he or she would continue.

By the New Kingdom dividing the body, soul and spirit had

reached its most complex. In her book, Egyptian Magic, the Golden Dawn occultist Florence Farr classed these bodies in the terms[3] that are familiar to modern occultists.

1. Kat, physical body.
2. Sahu, Astral body.
3. Tet, Spiritual body.
4. Khaibt, the Aura.
5. Hati, the habits and hereditary body (a similar idea to DNA).
6. Ab, the animal self or the heart.
7. Ka, the human ego.
8. Ba, the mental link to the divine.
9. Khoukhu, magical powers of the Soul
10. Hammemit, the unborn soul.

According to the obelisk of Queen Hatshepsu (around 1200BC), a human Hammemit circled the Sun for 120 years before various astrological and elemental forces drew it into incarnation. These forces gave the Hammemit a personality and destiny and encouraged a Sahu formed in the womb. Within this, the Hati inserted itself and together they formed a template for the Kat. The more energetic aspects of the Sahu withdraw to the perimeters of the Kat and become the Khaibt.

According to the obelisk, at birth, the Hammemit creates a double of the baby, which is called a Ka. The Ka links itself to the Hati by another body called the Ab (heart). The Egyptians believed the heart was the source of human wisdom, as well as emotions, memory, the soul and the personality. The heart through various channels linked all parts of the body together. These channels moved blood, air, saliva, mucus, sperm, nutriment and excrement around the body.

Farr said the Khoukhu was the magical power of the soul. The Khoukhu started nearly all magical acts both good and evil. As a result, the Khoukhu developed into a good or evil shape for all eternity. The Khoukhu had the power to chat to the unborn souls

---

[3] *Egyptian Magic*, Florence Farr, Aquarian Press, Wellingborough, 1982

and could take any form they pleased.   Other than the focus on magic, many of the attributions of the Khoukhu are similar to the Ank (which goes unmentioned by Farr). The Khoukhu is tested and tried after death and they journey to the underworld.

The inconsistency is fair, as the Egyptians never had a consistent definition of the parts of the body. The Ba and the Akh, for example, were often mixed-up.

During our period it is uncertain what the Ancient Egyptians believed, some Egyptologists think that for throughout the Pre-dynastic period and much of the Old Kingdom ordinary people thought that only the Pharaoh had a Ka, Ba, or Akh. They think the Pharaoh incorporated his people within his own soul and if he made so did they. This was why in the Old-Kingdom Egyptians worked on the pyramid complexes, to make sure their Pharaohs got into the Kingdom of Ausar and they could join them. However, there is evidence to suggest otherwise. It was only the rich and powerful that were given permission to build Mastaba tombs close to the pyramid tomb of Pharaoh. This was an echo of the old practice of killing the king's servants, courtiers to escort the dead king after his death – a practice which may have happened in the 1st and 2nd dynasties. The rituals surrounding death changed with the end the Old Kingdom. Death became more democratic and the rituals were increasingly available to anybody who had the money (in the Egyptian language, the term for extreme poverty was "he who has no money for his tomb"). By the New Kingdom, ready-made texts for the Pert-Em-Heru, with spaces for names were available from scribes.

 The oldest texts to mention the Ka is the "Pyramid Texts" on the fifth dynasty pyramid of Unas at Saqqara. At the same time, there were nobles' tombs that make it plain that at least the nobility were concerned about caring for their Kau (which is the plural) too.

Bas and other parts of the body do not get a mention in these tombs possibly because the belief in these elements of the afterlife did not develop until later. The "Coffin Texts" of the Middle Kingdom mention such entities as the Ka, Ba, and Akh as "personal" spirits rather than parts of the body.

Throughout this book we will be saying the pre-dynastic Egyptians each believed they had a Ka and a Ba and something like a divine body that evolved through life, went through trials and was judged after death. This divine body, whether called an Akh or a Khoukhu, had special powers, which, if refined, was a powerful force for good. This is our true spiritual self, our Higher Self and the divine force behind our incarnation.

Although there is little in the way of evidence for this view, it is unlikely the other developments would have happened if there were no source for them. That source is likely to have been from existing pre-dynastic beliefs.

From the view of the Egyptian shaman, the first task would be to make sure that his Ka, Ba and Akh were ready to work on all the spiritual levels needed. To do this they would have to make sure they could breathe properly.

The Book of Breathing

In the Egyptian Book of the Dead and the much later 'Book of Breathing' there were spells designed to make sure the dead person could breathe in the afterlife. These are odd spells because the Ancient Egyptians must have known the dead did not need 'air'. We have to look at this as symbolic. Ancient people saw breath as a sign of life and it was a sign that you had adapted to your environment. For example, you cannot breathe underwater, adaptation in this element is impossible and you may not live there.

The same applies to trance and near death states.

These are important for the Egyptian shaman because their trances were closer to a death state. The spells given in the Book of the Dead and the Book of Breathing are exercises which are designed to make changes in the various spiritual bodies. These helped a person adapt to the new spiritual environment in which they would now need to work.

The Book of Breathing suggests three areas of purification that must be performed before a person can exist in the spiritual realms. These are purifying the heart, front, back and midsection.

On one hand this sounds like the usual cleaning that is part of the mummification process however one sentence adds "no part of you is involved in wrongdoing" suggests there is more to it. What this is saying is that your heart, past and present is free from wrongdoing. This is important because on the astral realms of the shaman you see first through a mirror of yourself. What you want on the astral realms will come to you, good or bad, as like attracts like on the astral. Someone who has low self-esteem will continually meet patterns that emphases their lack of power. Those who wish to harm others will find those entities of violence drawn to them.

Purification of the self and strengthening of the self is the first stage of the Shaman and is a process that never stops.

The Book of Breathing hints at a rite that will help. It talks of cleaning your midsection soda and Natron. In mummification, Natron is a natural salt and when mixed with soda it preserves flesh by drying it out. You are removing the waters of chaos that bring about destruction.

Then there is a complex formula. It tells you should be purified in that pool of the Field of Offerings. Next, the gods Wadjet and Nekhbet must purify you. Then your body should be purified in the Hall of Geb and your body in the Hall of Shu. You see Re when he sets, Atum will be with you in the evening and give breath to you. Ptah rebuilds your body and then you are ready to enter the Neshmet ship with Ausar.

Unlocking this formula is not difficult. The field of offerings was the place of sacrifice. To the Ancient Egyptians this meant you had to pay your dues to the Gods. In modern terms, you have to be prepared to accept a divine being (or several) as an agency in your life. It seems like a contradiction in terms to think of an agnostic or atheistic shaman. However, there are those who believe they can wander through the paths of mysticism and magic without recognising something bigger than themselves. The Book of Breathing is saying to such people you will not even get past first base.

The gods Wadjet and Nekhbet were the protector goddesses of Upper and Lower Egypt from archaic times. What the book of breathing is suggesting here is that you have act out your responsibilities as a citizen of the society you are living. It is important to remember the Ancient Egyptian was mostly politically conservative. The law of the land reflected Divine Law (as expressed by the Goddess Ma'at). Crime and disharmony upset the rule of law and threw the world out of balance.

Rituals helped to restore that balance, as did acts of goodness. It is clear the path of the Egyptian shaman is not that of a radical, it is the one of restoring balance. This is not to say the Egyptian Shaman does not work to bring about change in their society for good, it is just they always do it within their society. Helping to heal the land from humanity's exploitation of it is the Shaman's work, as is conservation work and protecting animals and forests. Rioting against globalisation or sending pipe bombs to those who are involved with animal experiments is not.

The next section of the Book of Breathing appears to describe some ceremony. The Hall of Geb is the Earth. Geb was a nature god from pre-dynastic times. What this is suggesting is that you are purified by an experience in nature. Nu was the God of the Air and it seems this ceremony involves the rising (Re) and setting sun (Atum or Tem). Because of this experience, Ptah rebuilds the astral bodies so you can begin your shamanic journey.

This ceremony is hard work and in some ways would be easier for a dead person who has led a good life to achieve. To someone who is still living, it is an initiation and the beginning of your path as an Egyptian Shaman.

The Ceremony of Purification

This ceremony requires you to find some space where you can see the rising and setting sun. The best place is on a mountain where you cannot be seen by anyone else and so I recommend a camp-out. However, a city park is another choice if this is not possible but you are going to have to get there before the sun rises and many are closed now. You will need about a fistful of salt (not sea salt) which you mix with four teaspoons of bicarbonate of soda and a large bowl of water.

Check on the internet to find out what time sun is rising in your area and make sure that you are awake and in position half an hour earlier. Select a spot where you are unlikely to be disturbed, but where you can see the rising Sun.

Before sunrise, dissolve the bicarbonate of soda and the salt into the water. Stand and face east. Count five paces forward from the place where you will sit. Walk in a circle four times around the place you sit and sprinkle the water and soda to the left and the right. Then sit in the position of the seated shaman and wash yourself in the water. Then say the following four times.

> *"Oh Ausar, everything which is hateful in me has been carried away for thee. Tehuti has taken that which was uttered in the name of evil away to Ausar. I have brought that which was spoken in my name and have placed it in the palm of his hand. I shall not be separated from you, and you shall not be separated from me. Thy holy essence is in me for now and evermore."*

As you say this, you should imagine the god of the Moon and magic Tehuti appearing before you. You should see him reach into you and take a shadow of you and to carry it away to Ausar in the Underworld.

As the sun rises, you should stand and breathe in through the nose and out through the mouth. It should be regular, perhaps even the four two breath, but should be made with the accompanying visualisation.

Imagine yourself getting bigger until your can touch the vault of heaven. In your mind's eye reach out and touch the blue so it ripples as if you were touching water.

See Re on his boat above your head and say.

> *"I am Nu I draw air from the presence of the Light-god."*
> *From the utmost limits of heaven,*
> *From the utmost limits of earth,*
> *From the utmost limits of the sky.*
> *May air be given to me!"*

See a beam of light come from Re and breathe it into yourself. As you breathe out feel any weaknesses, illnesses, be breathed out with it. Feel that all the light from all of creation is being breathed into your body and out again. Do not speed up or slow down your breathing. It should remain natural. Do this for at least 10 breaths or until you cannot take the state of consciousness any longer.

Then say:

"My Body is purified
My Ka is purified
My Ba is purified
My Akh is purified"

Open your mouth and say:

"My mouth is open, I see with my eyes."

Images will come flooding into your mind. These will be some of your first shamanic experiences. Note them but do nothing else as this stage. Then allow yourself to become aware of your surroundings and note down your experiences.

Creating the House of Geb

The rite is the first stage of the purification. However, the Book of Breathing mentions another initiation, which is the experience of the House of Geb. Geb was the Earth god. The Egyptians tell the story of how Geb loved the star goddess Nut so much their coupling prevented her giving birth to other gods. To fix this problem the sky god Shu got between them, separated them, and allowed her to give birth. Geb constantly yearns for Nut.

He is shown as a naked man with an erection, which means that he is the raw power of nature. 'Building' the House of Geb is experiencing this raw power.

As before, you should go to a place in nature. Do not try the ceremony at night because it is easier during bright sunlight. It is easier during spring and early summer, when the trees start to draw energy from the ground and it is easier to feel and, if you are mildly psychic, see.

The ceremony

Dissolve the bicarbonate of soda and the salt into the water. Stand and face east. Count five paces forward from the place where you will sit. Walk in a circle four times around the place you sit and sprinkle the water and soda to the left and the right. Then light an incense stick and say the following rubric to the East, South, West and North while drawing the eye of Heru:

Eye of Heru
"The Eye of the Hawk shall protect the House of Geb"

Now wrap yourself in your blanket (leaving your head exposed), lie on your back in the centre and look at the sky. Relax, but do not shut your eyes. Regulate your breathing. Picture yourself as sinking into the ground. Feel your body merge with the earth. Do this slowly.

Slowly expand yourself so you can feel that you are part of a small part of the earth. Become aware of the plants that are growing on you. Move your consciousness into them.

Expand yourself still further until you begin to you are all the surface of the earth. You are aware of forests, mountains, flowing rives and oceans and creatures living and moving on you. When you have achieved this say aloud at least once:

"I am Geb and I dwell in my house"

Be aware of the sky and beyond the watery 'sea' of the star goddess that surrounds the earth. Look through the sky into the stars. Look on the galaxy with love and desire. Feel your energy driving upwards towards the stars. As you breathe out you drive the energy of the earth upwards.

You feel the feet of a huge being on your chest. Looking up you see a large bearded figure standing on you. This is the sky god Shu and he hold up the sky and prevents your energy spiralling out into space.

Shu looks at you and breathes. A gentle divine wind caresses your face. You breathe in, and the spiritual air invigorates your atoms and indeed that of the whole earth. Now say:

"I am Geb and my body has been purified by Shu."
I am Geb and Shu has purified my Ka
I am Geb and Shu has purified my Ba
I am Geb and Shu has purified my Akh
I breathe the breath of the Earth
And I am awakened"

Close your eyes and allow yourself to fall into trance. Just allow symbols and images to appear before you. Just note them for now. After a while, allow yourself to return to normal consciousness. Do not move away too quickly because you might find yourself getting too dizzy and feeling out of focus.

The final ceremony

We have now completed two important ceremonies. The final ceremony in sequence should be performed within a month of the last one. This is because we have been building up a pressure within the energy of our bodies. It is important to direct that energy as soon as possible. This phase, the ceremony will rebuild the energy fields in your body, strengthening it and enabling trance work to be performed easily.

This ritual will need you to be at your sacred spot at sunset. Go out to a place where you can see the setting sun on your face.

Look at the sky. Do not think of it as air, but as the surface of a great river. Without looking directly on it, see the sun, not as a ball of gas, but as a living God riding a boat on the surface of this river (If the sky is clouded you will have to imagine this).

> *"I send my voice to you oh eternal spirit Tem.*
> *Tem who goes down to the Tuat to bring light to dark places.*
> *Bring the light of your spirit until me as enter the dark and the land of dreams."*

Lie down, in the birth position wrap yourself in your blanket. Close your eyes quieten your mind and feel life awakening around you. When you are relaxed, mentally say:

> *"I send out my voice to Great Ram. I invite you to this place Atum. I welcome you to me, to bring me your mighty breath."*

In your mind's eye, visualise a Great Ram come to you. Feel its powerful energy. It breathes on you and something inside your heart lights up. Atum has awakened that divine spark within you. Quietly thank Atum and he leaves you. Now say:

> *"I send out my voice to the Great Ptah. I invite you to this place Ptah. I welcome you to me, to rebuild me in the image of Maat."*

Picture a figure of the God Ptah standing above you. In his hand is a wand that he points at you. Energy flows into you. You feel things inside you start to change. This will make you feel strange, even nauseous, however keep your mind focused on the divine spark which Atum has lit within your heart. When he has finished, Ptah will leave.

Allow yourself to listen to the spark that is in your heart. Know that when you open your eyes you will be seeing the world in a new way. Move your head out of your blanket. As you move yourself out of the birth position and slowly become aware of this time, space and reality, you are a new being.

Preparation of Inner Space

In my book 'Magical Pathworking', I described the process of building an Inner Kingdom. This essentially involved the use of imagination to build a space from where you could journey onwards. Because this space was the first place an inner voyager would go on their journey it reflect their subjective world rather than any inner reality. Rather than being a handicap, the shaman can use this place as a way of understanding their own psychological makeup. They can use it as the basis of the important magical assumption of the Egyptian godforms, which was a key part of a Shaman's work.

To perform this exercise takes some time and is worth taking some care over. You can use it as part of your own personal healing work. It is an important first base for any serious inner journey work. Building it clearly means that if you ever get lost, scared or disorientated during your inner journeys you have a safe place to return to.

So you should chose a simple word of power that will instantly focus your inner awareness to this place. Vibration of this word, which could be anything, will cause a picture of this place to appear in your mind. This of course has a practical implication in the spirit world, which is created by your higher mind. Once this reality is set up it will be possible to step back to this place and from there into this time and this reality.

The first time you visit this space you will need to ask for a spirit to be the hut's guardian. The first time you visit the hut, it should be seen as being unprotected. The more times you visit this space the more powerful the guardian will become.

First you should prepare your sacred space. Sit cross-legged and light a candle in front of you. Vibrate the name of power that you have chosen. Then allow the following images to appear in your mind.

Your are standing by the bank of the palm shaded river Nile. Look at your feet. You are wearing primitive sandals and are standing on black earth made fertile by the annual flooding of the Nile. You are wearing a single piece of woven cloth and around your shoulders is a leopard skin cloak. It is warm.

You turn around and behind you is a bustling village made of mud brick. You walk into the centre of the village and find a large round central hut that dwarfs all the others. As you approach it you notice a tingling of energy. It is as if a spirit is testing you to see if you are worthy to enter the hut. You say the name of the spirit and slowly it appears before you and stands aside. Try to see the spirit more clearly. It is by this act that you will make it grow stronger.

Enter the hut. In the centre is a fire. Before it is a skin on which you sleep and are the starting point of any journey that you may make. Lining the North and Western walls are shelves with tiny statues of the different gods and goddesses. There are pots full of various herbs and natron. There is a table on which are the remains of a meal. There is a small wooden box, which contains your material wealth. In the South there are four simple stone altars, one is for the Ancestors and one is for your village, the other is for the land and the last one is for you.

Sit on the skin before the fire. This is your space where you commune with the Gods and the ancestors.

The Shaman Hut

I mentioned the hut and the village will be a reflection of your own inner state. Therefore you should interpret what you see symbolically, as if it were a dream. All the symbols will relate to you, they will not mean anything to anyone else. For example if you see a dead duck in your path between the Nile and your hut, the symbol represents something blocking you which is symbolised by that bird. It does not relate to your Mother-in-Law even if you were going into the spirit journey with the idea of healing her.

The village does represent the people around you, but again only in the form they relate to you. You will see family members, friends and workmates. You will see them interact with each other, and it will show you how you see them and how they treat you. If you see someone that looks like your partner sneaking off to have an affair with your best friend, it does not mean that you are psychically picking up on something. It means that you are secretly, or not so secretly, insecure about your relationship. We will get to distant seership a little later.

The hut represents your physical body. It should be in a good state of repair. You should note if there are any holes as this might suggest where you have any physical illnesses. The treasure box will show the state of your finances. You will not find money in there, currency had not been invented in pre-dynastic Egypt, but instead you will find something symbolic of the state of your wealth.

The fire in the centre represents your own spiritual fire. In the east this is called Kundalini, it should be strong and warm, but it should not be out of control. The meal is the state of your domestic life. The Gods, Goddesses and herbs we will be using as magical tools later. The altars are to help you provide medicine to the various aspects the altar's represent.

It is important that you do not just see this hut as an imaginary place somewhere in your head. You should not only accept the place as being as real as this one, but you should make an effort to try to imagine the hut as occupying the same place as you are performing your shamanic work. It is worthwhile that after you have proved the inner reality of your shaman's hut, you open your eyes and imagine it surrounding you in this world. Once you get good at this, you should hear the sounds of the Nile in the distance with your physical ears, and should feel the fire which will be in front of you.

Calling for the Spirit of the Hut

This will require your first spirit quest. Fortunately you do not have to go far. You should prepare sacred space and wrap yourself in your blanket. Vibrate the name of power that you will use to activate the inner space. First visit your hut and imagine yourself sitting in front of the fire cross-legged. Say out loud

> "I send my voice to the horizon from which Re goes forth. Mighty Hor, place me under thy wings of protection. Place me under the power of thy mighty eye. For as I thrive, so shall ye. Take me to the place where I might find a guardian spirit to live with me."

Allow yourself to rise through the roof of the hut. See the village moving below you. Higher you rise until you are surrounded by clouds. After a while the clouds will clear and you will find yourself in a new landscape. Wait for a spirit to come to you. It might be in the form of a human or animal. Although you might see many things it will be the first one that approaches you. When you see it you should say:

> *"Thanks be to you, oh creature who does the bidding of Heru. Heru will not let you perish and he has set our foes under our feet. Come with me until the time that Heru bids you to leave. In the name Heru. Tell me thy name, so I may call you."*

The creature will tell you its name

Hold onto the creature and allow yourself and it to descend through the clouds and into your hut. You should feed the creature from the meal.

The creature will remain with you and provide you with protection. After a while, it will be decided that its work is done. It will somehow tell you this and you should journey with it to the land from where it came. You should thank it for its work. You should then immediately go back to your hut and ask Heru to provide you with another guardian.

Becoming a God

One of the most dramatic parts of shamanic work is assuming a spirit. There are two ways to do this, the safe and the unsafe way. I am going to tell you both so you can make up your mind to stick to the safe way.

The unsafe way is the method that shamans have used for millenniums. It involved allowing the spirit to take control of their body. The spirit would then dance or perform some magical act. They would do this until the shaman could effectively throw them out of his body and take charge again. The obvious risk is that some spirits are less willing to leave and are inclined to stick around. In Ancient times a shaman could be locked-in their hut or allowed to charge throw the undergrowth in madness. However this is a little tricky when the shaman has to be at work the next day. Modern work practices do not tolerate possession of their employees by Ancient deities or spirits who often have a lack of ability to perform modern duties adequately.

The technique involved is similar to a medium during a Trance. The shaman would get themselves into a deep altered state, call the being and stand aside while the spirit takes control of their body. It is hard to do, because even the most psychic person always leaves a part of themselves behind in the body. This sees the spirit as an alien and will often try to repel it. The presence of this remaining part of the self will be what the spirit will need to use the body, speak or move about. If it manages to achieve this, then the way that it will act is coloured by the personality of the shaman. The spirit will use knowledge that it finds in the person's memory to communicate. This is alright if the person has a large pool of knowledge, memories or experience. It is lousy if the spirit cannot find the intellectual language to communicate effectively. For example a shaman might find that a god is talking about love all the time. This is mostly because the intense power and emotion they are experiencing feels like love to them. It might not be the perspective of the spirit.

Ancestors are the most dangerous things to allow the deep trance possession we are describing here. This is because they only represent the personality, rather than the spirit, of the ancestor. Some of them are inclined to hang on to the shaman rather than continue to allow the natural process of the personality to decay after death.

Ancestors often give unreliable advice anyway because it is coloured by the views of the shaman's knowledge of history. A person who channelled an ancestor once claimed to me that Julius Caesar once was able to rally his troops who could see his 'long curly golden hair'. This would have been a great relief to Caesar who was bald and, when he had hair, it was dark. Alexander the Great however was famous for his blonde hair, so the medium must have confused the two people.

Modern Shamanic work has borrowed techniques from the various esoteric schools such as the Hermetic Order of the Golden Dawn which makes this a little safer. These techniques include something called 'Godform assumption'. This involves imagining an image of the God or Goddess as a tiny statue.

1. Picture yourself as becoming transparent
2. Placing the small statue inside your body around your groin area.
3. Call for the God or Goddess to come to you
4. See a light above your head, like a star.
5. Draw this light, through your body where it connects to the statue, making it live.
6. Allow the statue to grow until it is as high as your eyes.
7. Make mind to mind contact with the God or Goddess.

By keeping the deity smaller than yourself, you are keeping control of the being and preventing it from taking you over. If ever you feel threatened, you can withdraw your consciousness from the statue, disconnect the light from the statue and force it to shrink. You can then remove it from your aura.

Remember the little statues of the Gods and Goddesses which are in the shamans hut? If you try doing your godform assumption work there, you can take the statue out off-the-shelf and then afterwards put it back. This will help you to reduce some of the effects of godform assumption.

It is possible to make anything into a godform. You could use an animal spirit, ancestor, God or Goddess.

Things you can do with a Godform

Speak

People who have assumed a godform can pick up a sense of the right thing to say in connection to that being. In the years I have worked with them, I find the literal information which comes from channelling godforms needs to be taken with a heart-stopping-sized pinch of salt. This is mostly because, unlike mediumship where the person has given over control to the godform, the personality is alive, loud and kicking. The unconscious mind, which is usually suppressed, is given a medium in which it is allowed to speak. If it feels it is being taken seriously it will overwhelm any energy being given off by the Godform and speak its mind.

Dance

The idea of dancing the godform comes from shamanism. It is a way of mixing the divine energies with your own and allowing them to manifest in this world. It is true when you are mediating Animal godforms, which do not speak and teach by the way they move.

Dancing was an important part of Ancient Egyptian worship. During the pre-dynastic period archaeologists have found depictions of female figures, perhaps of Goddesses or Priestesses, dancing with their arms raised above their heads. The act of dancing was an important ingredient of ritual and celebration in Ancient Egypt.

One example were the Muu-Dancers, these wore kilts and reed crowns and danced in a goose step at funeral processions. It seems they might have been a remnant of shamans whose job it was to follow the dead person to the Otherworld.

During the Old Kingdom they are shown wearing papyrus fronds emerging from the tops of their heads and they dance with their thumbs and index fingers extended from closed fists. This was a magical gesture designed to protect from nasties like crocodiles and snakes. They are guardians of the necropolis and must approve any burials.

According to the archaeologist Hartwig Altenmeller[4], the dancers are probably representing the 'people of Pe', who were the ferrymen of the dead mentioned in the Pyramid texts. Their odd goose step is a suggestion they are walking between the worlds, which is an important role for a shaman. You can imagine that before the funeral service, a group of shaman would spend the night in the dead person's tomb. After assuming the godforms of the ferrymen, they would carry the dead person to the otherworld. They would then dance their powers into the earth to make sure the dead person would travel smoothly to Amenti.

---

[4] *Untersuchungen zu alt?gyptischen Bestattungsdarstellungen* (Gl_ckstadt/Hamburg, 1963) You can read a fascinating article on the Muu dancers by Greg Reeder [http://www.egyptology.com/reeder/muu/]

Rituals

One of the most important uses of godform assumption is as a tool to improve ritual. This was the idea of the ancient shaman and the later Egyptian magicians. We have many magical manuscripts that suggest that many long invocations carried out by magicians were help them see themselves as the God form they were hoping to use to heal.

For example this spell that was designed to help a magician contact the spirit of a dead person might read :

> "Open my eyes
> Open thy eyes
> Open Tat
> Open Nap
> For I am Artamo… the great basilisk of the east
> I rise in glory with my father at dawn.
> Oh Ibis sprinkle thy wings on the waters
> Which are my eyes to the otherworld
> So I may see the great God Anu"[5]

Another famous god form invocation is that of Ausar which is still used to day by the Hermetic Order of the Golden Dawn and was lifted from the Book of the Dead.

> For I am Ausar Triumphant, even Ausar on-Nophris, the Justified:
> I am He who is clothed with the Body of Flesh,
> Yet in whom is the Spirit of the Great Gods:
> I am The Lord of Life, triumphant over Death.
> He who partaketh with me shall arise with me:
> I am the Manifestor in Matter of Those Whose Abode is the Invisible:
> I am purified: I stand on the Universe:
> I am the Reconciler with the Eternal Gods:
> I am the Perfector of Matter:

---

[5] This is a paraphrase of a spell in the Leyden Papyrus, see *The Demotic Magical Papyrus of London and Leiden*, FLI Griffith and Herbert Thompson, 1904, H Grevel and Co, London.

And without me, the Universe is not.'

Once a person assumes the godform and makes these sorts of invocations, the godform becomes a natural part of them. Its energy can be focused and projected into talismans, or to heal someone. We will be looking at this later.

Chapter Three

Ancient Percussion and Chant

So far we have relied on meditative techniques to reach the necessary trance states. Ancient Shamans relied on other methods to reach deeper states much quicker. Ancient humanity discovered that certain vibrations and sounds had different effects on them. Many of these vibrations they could control either by playing musical instruments or chanting at certain pitches.

Neolithic people build their tombs and temples to strengthen their voices and increase the intensity of vibrations. The megalithic chamber at New Grange in Ireland, for example, has been built to reflect sound waves at a particular resonance. This intensified the sound until it had a physical quality. Some scientists think many of the geometric swirls painted on such tombs might be pictures of these sound waves. The sound makers saw these symbols as they chanted in the smoke-filled chambers.

The technology is not exactly rocket science. The same ideas go into building a modern stereo speaker. You will probably know that in a modern stereo speaker size is not everything and it is possible to get a deep bass sound from a small set of speakers. This is because the box controls the reverberation of the bass frequency and make it more intense. You can also make a difference to the sound yourself by putting your speakers in corners or on hollow box[1].

Later temple designers in Greece, Malta and Egypt had bass frequencies in mind too. Not only do the rooms cause much echo they contain stone boxes and altars that would make it even more intense.

---

[1] An audiophile will run screaming from the room if you do this, so I would advise this experiment be conducted when you don't have one in the house.

British occultist, Marian Green, told me how she, with a group of her students, experimented with a chant in a Minoan temple in Crete. The impact the sound had nearly knocked them over.

One of the magical powers deep bass sounds have is that if they are low enough your ear cannot tell which direction they come from. If you have ever been to a rock concert where the artist has spent money on a decent stereo, it is possible to feel a pure bass sound coming at you from all directions. A friend of mine is an audiophile who insists that bass frequencies roll across the floor from his expensive speakers. He likes this effect so much that he lies down to listen to his music.

It is likely the ancients had the same feeling about by the vibration that bass sounds make. The purer the bass sound, the less vibration of other objects it creates. You can tell a bad stereo by the extent the bass causes the floor and walls to vibrate.

My audiophile friend used to play his stereo loud. One night there was a knock on the door from his neighbour. He thought that she had come to complain about the noise. She had, but not from his stereo. Another neighbour was playing a cheap Radio and the distorted sound could be heard while his louder stereo could not.

Bass frequencies represent those deep subconscious stirrings that we normally keep under wraps. By playing bass oriented sounds we stir those automatic parts of ourselves. Like the bass notes themselves which are often below the frequency the human ear can hear, we are often unaware of these impulses but they are the driving force behind our lives. However impressive this may be, bass is not the only sound-based magical effect. Midrange and high Frequency sounds are also important.

Midrange sounds, such as the pitch of a normal voice, focus our minds on the physical word while high frequency sound shifts our attention to the spiritual realms.

Imagine you are a Neolithic villager entering a sacred barrow or temple. You know that such places were meeting places between humanity and the spirits. There would be the strange smell of burned herbs and the air would be thick with smoke. You would enter a room and the shaman from would start a deep chant. You would not be able to tell which direction the chant was coming from and the vibrations would be so intense the smoke in the barrow would form into patterns.

The hair on the back of your neck would stand on end as you feel the bass stir your unconscious. You might feel fear, after all you are in a place where dead spirits live. Or you might feel the stirrings of physical power as the sound unlocks the drives of your being.

A priest would take that energy by calling the gods. The regular chant of his voice and the earthly requests he makes takes the bass notes and raises it upwards, controlling it and directing it towards a purpose, giving it clarity of direction. There is a rattle of bells and a single female voice singing a high note. Suddenly the air is alive with spirits. The voices continue as the sounds mix and merge in the rarefied atmosphere. More shapes form in the smoke and these are the physical signs the spirits were among them.

This symphony of sound was part of the process the shaman would use to link the worlds. Even if this were not magical enough, there is increasing evidence the sound has an affect on your brain waves.

The Brain reacts to sound

Your brain is not where you think. You actually think in many of the subtle bodies that make up those energy fields that surround your physical body. Your brain is a link between those energy fields and your body. It takes the images from the senses and make sure it goes to the right place for interpretation. Modern science is at the point where it can see where the various parts of the brain fire and convert these electrical currents. It has not reached the point where it can see what it does next because modern science has a problem when it comes to looking at objects like the aura. But it seems the brain decodes the frequencies of the five senses and converts them into something we can use. As we have seen sound is a frequency and your brain will respond to it as if it were a physical object.

In the last few years various fringe scientists have been peddling tapes that contain sounds at certain frequencies that they say will create an effect in the brain. They are also specific about what frequency will cause a specific effect. For example on one tape a sound at 6.5Hz will create a feeling of unity and speeded up language ability while 7 Hz will induce astral projection and bend spoons! It would be good if this was possible, but the brain and the personality is unique and everybody's frequencies are slightly different. Also if it were true then an evening listening to your stereo could result in confusion and most of your cutlery getting tied in knots.

However, the theory is correct. Sound does stimulate different brain waves. Although I want to avoid getting too technical the human ear can hear sound starting at the low 20Hz and ending at the high 20,000 Hz.

The brain also works on similar energy cycles and these brain waves are like broad categories of how fast your brain is working. There are five main brain wave patterns.

- Alpha, which is when we are relaxed.
- Beta, when we are awake and alert
- Gamma, which is when we are stressed or alert.
- Theta, when we are in near sleep
- Delta, when we are in a coma or deep sleep.

Delta speed is anything lower than three hertz, Theta is three to seven Hertz, Gamma is more than 30 Hertz, Beta is between 13-30 Hertz and Alpha is between eight to 12 Hertz.

These speed limits are similar to the speeds of bass sound, which is why people thought if you played these frequencies then your brain would automatically shift to that state of consciousness. The problem is that most of the ranges would be below what the ear can hear, so you would not be aware of them. The argument of the tape people is that it does not matter and your brain picks up the vibration anyway. This would be a good excuse except such tapes are heard on headphones which cannot play deep frequencies anyway. My stereo speakers (which are not a bad) can only play bass notes higher than 40Hz.

Also since most of the sound around us is above the frequency ranges of our brain waves it would constantly be driving us more and more awake.

Even if it was somehow feeling the lower ranges of sound, the brain must be taking the average certain specific patterns. Bass sounds push it towards the alpha, delta and theta ranges while the higher ranges stimulate the brain into the higher more agitated states. The brain averages out mixed sounds, such as those we have in our ordinary life. So a piece of rock music might have slightly more bass which would normally relax us (alpha state), but mixed with a screeching electric guitar (gamma state) it would average us into a normal awake (beta) state.

A writer for example knows there are certain types of music they can listen to when they write. Some music will destroy their concentration others will stimulate it.

In 1973, Gerald Oster, of Mt. Sinai Medical Centre, published a paper called "Auditory Beats in the Brain". He noticed that if you play a frequency in one ear and a different one in another your brain resonates at a frequency that is the difference between the two tones.

So if you hear a sound that at 50Hz and another at 60hz your brain will resonate at 10hz. This third "beat" is called a binaural beat and was the key to getting your brain to work at the state you wanted.

It was impossible for our Ancient Egyptian shaman to know this. However they probably did know that if they chanted at a certain frequency while playing an instrument, or banging a drum at another they would find it easier to get into the state they wanted. They also knew that some instruments worked better for them than others.

Clues to Ancient Egyptian Magical Music

From archaeology, tomb paintings and engravings we know the Ancient Egyptian used Voice, Chanting, Hand clapping, Wooden sticks, castanets, drums, rattles, systrums, small bells and harps. Early shamanic magic must have incorporated them. Rebuilding sacred music and chant based on such evidence is like looking at a picture of a rock band playing and working out the chords of Stairway to Heaven.

However we do have a few other clues in the Ethiopian and Coptic Churches. These churches, which cut themselves off from the Greek Orthodox church early on in Church history carry out many rites that would be familiar to the Ancient Egyptians.

One of which included bearing the Ark from the temple. They carry it among the people in much the same way as the statues of the Egyptian Gods were. Priests carry sistria which were Ancient Egyptian rattles dedicated to Hathor and Aset and drums. Blind cantors teach the traditional chants. The use of professional blind singers was common in pharaonic temples. The famous hymn "Kyrie Eleison" may have descended from prayers to Atum, the sun god. Some of Coptic hymns mention Egyptian towns that have not existed for millenniums and are fragments of song's originally sung to the Ancient Gods.

If the fragments of temple music and chant are found in the Coptic or Egyptian Orthodox Church, what does this sound like? It is hard to describe. I recommend the reader visit a sacred music store and find live recordings. The closest estimation is that of a Gregorian, or traditional Orthodox chant, with an emphasis on the vowels and a trill which makes it sound Arabian. The technique involves drawing out the sound of a single vowel or syllable for long periods, with either regular or irregular rhythm. In the Hallelujah Hymn known as Offerato Ally, the first vowel covers three pages of music.

This is remarkably similar to the comments of the late Hellenistic writer Demetrius of Phalerum (345-283BC). In his treatise, 'De Eloutione' he says that vowel chanting was an important part of Egyptian religion in his day. He said:

> *"In Egypt the priests, when singing hymns in praise of the gods, employ the seven vowels which they utter in due succession and the sound of these letters is so euphonious that men listen to it in place of the flute and lyre"* [2]

It might seem strange to us that vowels could be considered so

---

[2] Fowden, Garth. The Egyptian Hermes: a historical approach to the late pagan mind. New York: Cambridge University Press, 1986. p 118.

important to the Egyptians, but you have to remember that their language didn't write them down. And given that they give the clue to pronouncing the word they are important.

According to the English musical historian Ernest Newlandsmith, who with the Egyptian Dr Ragheb Moftah spent a lifetime notating Coptic sacred music, once you pierced the veil of the tradition you found:

> *"The music is not Arabic, it is not Turkish and it is not Greek - often as these elements appear... It seems impossible to doubt but that this is Ancient Egyptian. Moreover, it is great music: grand, pathetic, noble and deeply spiritual."* [3]

There are other likenesses with the various tomb paintings and the Coptic church cantors. The facial characteristics and the way the orchestra conductor, gives a rhythm by his right hand on the knee while the left hand draws the melody in the air. Also the method used by the Coptic Cantors to vibrate sound while contracting their face nose and mouth muscles can be clearly seen in New Kingdom art.

Chant

One of the most effective and powerful shamanic techniques was the chant.

Chanting is a traditional practice within many spiritual paths, particularly those that have their roots in the native Middle Eastern traditions, such as Judaism and Sufism.

In the Eastern tradition chanting is called Mantra. It is when you select a phrase or word and repeat it until you no longer hear yourself doing it, until everything blurs and you find yourself in a spiritual awareness of what the word is or does. You can go on a spiritual journey that feels like you have been carried away for a long time and come back and find that you have been chanting the whole time.

---

[3] The Ancient Music of the Coptic Church, a lecture by Ernest Newlandsmith, University of Oxford, on May 21, 1931, (http://www.coptic.org/music/oxford.htm)

It works on two different levels. The first is the power of the words that are chant and the rhythmic effect the chanting.

Theoretically you could be able to chant 'jam sandwich' over and over and reach an altered state. However for some reason it does not work like that. The Eastern Tradition has a battery of them that are designed to reach special altered states or to open the various energy centres. The point is the word has to mean something spiritual or direct you to a special place. It can't do that if you don't believe in the power of the word and it is clear the Ancient Egyptians believed in the magical power of words. In fact the words Heka and Hu mean 'magic' and 'word' and were the gods that represented the creative power of the Gods.

In Dynastic times, Heka stands in the prow of the sun god Re's Boat of Millions of Years with Hu. In one of the legends after creating the universe, Re drew blood from his own penis and created the gods Hu and Sia (who represented Divine Knowledge). Heka, accompanied these two gods.

When Hu breathed out he made a sound that was like his name and when he did, the Gods were created. His first breath created Ausar and his last creation was the Sun. The Ancient Greeks would come to associated Hu with the word Logos, which was the word used in the first chapter of John's gospel when it says:

> *"In the beginning was the Word and the Word was with God and the Word was toward God; all things were made through him and without him and nothing was made without him. In him was life and the life was the light of men. The light that shineth in the dark and the darkness has not overcome it."*

It is an interesting point the Christian use of Logos can word for word be applied to the Ancient Egyptian to Hu, and the redemptive powers that they were to apply to their God Christ could be linked to him.

Hu acted as the King's companion as the King entered the Afterlife. Through Hu, the King upheld his royal authority in the Afterlife. The Ancient Egyptians believed the Sphinx was an image of Hu. Originally, until a human face was carved on it, the Sphinx was a lion.

The Ancient Egyptian's thought the word 'heka' meant a little more than magic too. In fact they saw it as Life Force itself. So words were regarded as divine and know the name of something meant to have power over it too.

So if the magic words were so important to the Ancient Egyptian, what did they use?

Unfortunately we can't be sure but we do have a few clues. In much later periods, when Egypt was under the control of the Greeks, there are many magical manuscripts that have magical names and chants on them. For example:

"Askei kataski eron oreon ior mega semnuor bauo," is chanted three times in one manuscript to invoke the Greek moon goddess Hekate. In another case, a name Phnounebeo, which is a God or Goddess, is chanted twice for protection.

Unfortunately we don't know if this method was a corruption of earlier magical practice or a Greco-Egyptian invention.

It is clear from the magic spells left to us, the names of the Gods and Goddesses were considered powerful. Not only did they have their public names, they also had secret names that effectively gave the person who knew it a hot line to the God or Goddess and power over them. We will look at how we gain these secret names later in this book. However at this point we can say that chanting these names will be a good way of linking yourself to those powers.

When the Ancient Egyptian's chanted the names of power or their Gods how did they do it? It is an important question because there are many different systems of chanting names in different traditions throughout the world. The North American Indian chant is different from that of the Tibetan monk and the Shaman of Siberia's long rolling vibration is different from the quiet muttering of the African snake charmers.

Looking again at the example of the Coptic cantors, the impression is that the Ancient Egyptians vibrated words and prolonged their vowels. The Western Mystery tradition vibrates chants as low as the voice can go feeling the heart of the sound as coming from inside the chest.

Coptic cantors' voices are not low. They make a vibration at the top of the roof of the mouth and the pitch is within the normal midrange rather than anything too deep. This gives a slightly more nasal sound than traditional chanting, but once you get the knack of it you can sing notes within a chant, which is harder to do with a deeper sound.

Practice

I have said the Egyptian Gods had descriptive names and these can be used as magical formulas. The one we are going to try with this exercise is Ptah-kehery-bak-ef. It means 'Ptah who is under his Moringa tree' and is meaningless to a modern person. However, Ptah, who is one of the earliest 'human' gods was the patron god of the city of Memphis. Memphis was one of the key cities of Early Egypt and so he became associated with the idea of rulership. Later he would become a creator god and the engineer of the Egyptian pantheon. Towards the end of the pre-dynastic period Ptah took over the roles of a tree God in Memphis. Although we are not sure of the name of this God or Goddess we know it was a Moringa (Horseradish) tree. Moringa's were a magical tree because the leaves, pods, seeds, flowers, and roots of the Moringa tree are edible and are packed full of vitamins and minerals. In fact they may have been used to as medicines to cure dietary disorders as the leaves are high in vitamin C of oranges, calcium, potassium, vitamin A and protein. The flowers were high in calcium and potassium. The Egyptians used the juice for cosmetic and fragrance preparation. It was supposed to act as a moisturiser.

So here we have the image of a ruling God under a magical tree of healing and beauty. If we hold this image in mind as you vibrate his name it will be interesting to see what you get.

Lie down, in the birth position wrap yourself in your blanket. Close your eyes quieten your mind and feel life awakening around you. When you are relaxed, mentally say:

Ancient Percussion and Chant

"I send my voice to you oh eternal spirit Ptah.
Ptah who stands under the Moringa Tree of Memphis.
Bring the me light of your spirit oh Ptah-kehery-bak-ef as I enter the dark and the land of dreams.
Come to me as I chant thy holy name."

Relax your mind and body. When your mind is as clear as possible, practice vibrating the words from the top of your mouth using your normal speaking voice. Pause and then take a deep breath. Then vibrate the word stressing the vowel sound so it is more like Taaaaaaaaar-keeeeeeeee-heeeeeeeer-reeeeeeeeee-baaaaaaark-eeeeeeeeeef. Keep repeating this to a regular rhythm. Do not allow yourself to go any faster or slower. It will take some time before anything happens but soon you will find yourself getting bored. Then you will find images coming into your mind. For now, push those images aside and keep concentrating on your chant. Then a strong image will arrive that will be harder to shake. Keep chanting but allow your imagination to follow where ever the image takes you.

When the journey is finished allow yourself to stop chanting, relax and become aware of the world around you.

Once you have the hang of chanting in monotone you can go up a note on the second to last syllable of each 'word' and then let it drop again. So it would sound like TaaaaaaaaAr-keeeeeeeEe-heeeeeeeEr-reeeeeeeeEe-baaaaaaaaRk-eeeeeeeeeEf. You must still keep the rhythm and so this becomes a harder but much more authentic method. If you want to get it accurate you turn the last part of the word into an Eastern trill. This is similar to the Moslem call to prayer and takes much practice. At time of writing I still could not control my voice well enough to do it. However it is not necessary. What is important is that you find the vibration point and keep it going.

Group Chant

Besides the chanting, it is clear the Ancient Egyptians used some form of call response chant. This is similar to the modern army where marching troops have their drill sergeant shout out a phrase and the troops reply. The script could go something like this:

> Sergeant: We are strong and we are tough
> Troops: We are strong and we are tough
> Sergeant: 'cause we eat our wheaty puffs
> Troops: 'cause we eat our wheaty puffs
> Sergeant: Wheaty puffs
> Troops: Wheaty puffs[4]
> Sergeant: Cornflakes
> Troops: Cornflakes

And then it starts over. This gave the soldiers a beat to keep them marching in step. It also provides a mantra to take the troops mind off marching. However according to one Old Kingdom tomb (about 2200 BC) a song could be sung between two groups for the same reasons. The song written on the tomb has a scene depicting sheep trampling seeds in the field. A supervisor is leading the chant, like the sergeant. The words are:

> Supervisor: "Oh, Western Goddess! Where is the shepherd?"
> Helpers: "The shepherd is in the water beneath the fish. He talks to the catfish and greets the mormry-fish."
> Supervisor: "Oh shepherd of the Western Goddess."[5]

While such a song loses much in the translation and we are left with no idea how it worked, it seems to be a common method of the time. It was to get workers moving together and take their mind off their backbreaking work in a similar method to the drill sergeant's rhyme.

This can get a group of people into an altered state effectively. Once on a male mysteries workshop a group of us armed with sticks (which we thumped on the floor to get a regular rhythm chanted something which was supposed to be an African warrior's chant. I have no idea if it was or not. But, after we had chanted it for an hour,

---

[4] Of course they wouldn't use these exact words, because that would be a bit silly.
[5] See 'Life of the Ancient Egyptians' Eugen Strouhal, 1992, University of Oklahoma Press

any wildebeest which happened to stray into Berkshire that evening was in grave danger of being clubbed to death by a bunch of half naked programmers, accountants and a journalist.

Something similar can be noted with the Maori haka[6] (war chant) which works on a similar principle. Ha-ka means "to ignite the breath". It is designed to energise the body and inspire the spirit. The haka was part of the Maori warrior's training for the culture's ritualised warfare. Many will be familiar with the hakas performed by the New Zealand rugby team, the All Blacks before they play a game. Although they look a bit silly, they are designed to scare the opponent. However this particular haka is nothing like the real thing being performed in context with something the Maori called mana[7]. When I was living in New Zealand, I visited a Maori college where 40 boys decided to perform the story of St Paul in the form of a haka. Because of all the ritualistic jumping about the audience sat on the stage, while the boys took up most of the hall. The wall of psychic force that came from the 'performers' was almost visible. It was not hate, in the same way that a lightning storm does not broadcast emotion, it was just raw power and a mortal standing in front of it just did not want to be there.

The words of such chants do not seem to be important. In fact the famous All Black haka is said like this (I have put a literal translation underneath it)

Leader
    KA MATE!   KA MATE!
    We're going to die!   We're going to die!

Chorus
    KA ORA,   KA ORA!
    We're going to live!   We're going to live!

---

[6] Compare this word with the Ancient Egyptian word Heka (magic word). It is not the only Maori word which is similar to Ancient Egyptian. The Maoris also worshiped a sun god called Re.

[7] No European has come up with a satisfactory translation of Mana. It is like prestige, power and 'face' all rolled into one.

Leader
>   KA MATE!   KA MATE!
>   We're going to die!   We're going to die!

Chorus
>   KA ORA,   KA ORA!
>   We're going to live! We're going to live!
>
>   TENEI TE TANGATA PU'RU-HURU
>   This is the man, so hairy
>
>   NA'A NEI TIKI   MAI WHAKA-WHITI TE …
>   who fetched,   and made shine the
>
>   … RE! HUPANE!   KA-UPANE!
>   sun! Upward step!   Another … !
>
>   A HUPANE!   KA-UPANE!
>   An upward step!   Another… !
>
>   WHITI TE RE!
>   The sun shines!
>
>   HI ! [8]

Applying the same idea to an Egyptian theme it is necessary to get a good rhythm, either by clapping, drumming or banging sticks on the ground. Once the leader has worked out the syllables of the words to the rhythm be can begin

> Leader: iai-ui em hetep
> Group: iai-ui em hetep
> Leader: iai-ui em hetep
> Group: iai-ui em hetep
> Leader: Ankh-k na
> Group: Ankh-k na

---

[8] This haka was written in 1810 by a very famous maori Chief Te Rauparaha who hid in a sweet potato (Kumara) pit when he was being chased by enemies. When he climbed out, he found someone standing over him who turned out to be an ally. Out of relief Te Rauparaha performed the haka.

Leader: : Neter Het-hert ankh-k na
Group: Neter Het-hert ankh-k na

This is a chant written in Ancient Egyptian as translated by the Egyptologist E.A Wallis Budge. It means "Come, come in peace, You have given me life, Goddess Hathor, you have given me life."

Here is another more traditional chant.. I have adapted a chant which was made before the shrine of Ausar, by the priestesses of Auset and Nephthys . After everyone had been purified, the priestesses, who must not have bare arms, crowned their heads with woollen scarves[9] .

> *Behold the lord Ausar! (Repeat four times the formula.)*
> *Praise be to his temple--great in heaven and earth (Repeat four times the formula.)*
> *He is the purified image of his father Tenen,*
> *He proceedeth from Tum,*
> *Perfect is he, like his father, the eldest god*
> *Let those among us who travel not thy path be embraced by thee:*
> *Beautiful of face and greatly beloved is the image of Tenen,*
> (Repeat the last verse four times)
>
> *Lo! The Bull, begotten of the two cows Auset and Nephthys!*
> *Lo! There cometh the bearer of the bronze-coloured sistrum, as the praises increase;*
> *Beautiful when he beholdeth him, the lord, among the seated ones,--*
> *He, the progeny of the two cows Auset and Nephthys,*
> *He appeareth unto us in thy image, like the one beloved.*
> *Travel thou among us, oh thou praised one,*
> *Raise us living in place of what thou hast made empty.*
> *Come thou in peace, oh our lord, whom we behold; our prince!*
> *Approach in peace; drive away tempest from before our temple;*
>
> *Send thy protection over us like a male protector* (Repeat the last line four times)

---

[9]The full version was translated in *The Burden Of Isis,* by James Teackle Dennis, London (1910)

Percussion

A drumbeat was used to coordinate the rhythms of oarsmen on the boats that sailed the Nile. This is important when you realise the Ancient Egyptians believed the Nile was sacred and connected to heaven and to the underworld. It is therefore likely the Pre-dynastic shaman would use his drum and the driving force into both those worlds.

Drumming is popular with modern shamans, who often use it as their main technique to get into an altered state. This is because the drum has a resonance and can alter brain waves and shift the person hearing them into an altered state quickly.

The Psychiatrist Carl Jung noted this effect when he joined a group of African drummers and dancers. As the drums started to take control he became overwhelmed by a primal fear. He was terrified of losing control and becoming mad like the drummers and dancers appeared to him. He ordered the drums away and has to beg and pay for them to move apart.

Finding a genuine pre-dynastic Egyptian's shaman's drum is a little tricky as we have to guess what one would be like. Most modern shamans use a frame drum, such as a Celtic Bodhrán (Bow-Rawn), mostly because they are light and give a good resonance when struck by a stick.

However In her book *When the Drummers were Women*, Layne Redmond, the round frame drum appears for the first time after our period during a ritual during the reign of Pharaoh Amenophis III, c. 1417 - 1379 BC.

Instead, a pre-dynastic shaman would probably have used a traditional African barrel-shaped drum made from hollowed tree trunks.

These are large, rounded and have animal skin or parchment on both ends. Sometimes a strip of catgut underneath the skin on both heads to give the effect of a snare drum. Commonly, the Egyptian drums were carried with the help of a shoulder strap. The long drum was struck on both heads with the hands while the early version of the snare drum was struck with sticks. Sticks are rarer and are usually associated with military snare drums.

Playing an African drum is an interesting experience, particularly if you are with a large group of people. Once you have all mastered the rhythm, it is possible to get carried away, even while you are playing. However it is much harder to do this by yourself. This means that for most people working by themselves it is nearly impossible to get yourself into an altered state without losing the rhythm. Some get around this by recording a rhythm and playing it back during their trance work. This is OK provided you are playing it back on a good quality stereo that has a low bass response.

There are many different theories about what is the best rhythm to use to get into an altered state. In my experience, most rhythms will take you out if you listen to them long enough. The drum feels like your heart beat. When you move fast your heart beats faster so if you have a rhythm which is too fast you will find your trance will also be too energetic. My first experiences with shamanism involved two beats, one slow and one fast. The slow beat was used for most of the trance while the fast one was when you wanted to hurry back afterwards. The slow beat would a beat every three quarters of a second and the fast one would two beats per second. It takes some experimentation to find out how fast you want to go during inner trance work. It is important to stick to the same beat for most the trance.

For those of you who have not experienced drumming as a method to get into an altered state, you are wondering how a noise that is one of the prime ingredients of rock music can help someone relax.

First the drum does not have the life walloped out of it. It is played softly. Second you do not listen to the beat directly. Instead you listen to the silence between the beats. After a while you will start to hear an echo, it sounds like silver bells. After a while of listening, your mind goes into a trance quickly. If you listen to rock music in this state you can also do the same thing. During the period I was experimenting with a lot with shamanism, I had a tendency to 'trip' to ordinary music and discos had a habit of becoming entranced stumbling about a bit like a zombie[10].

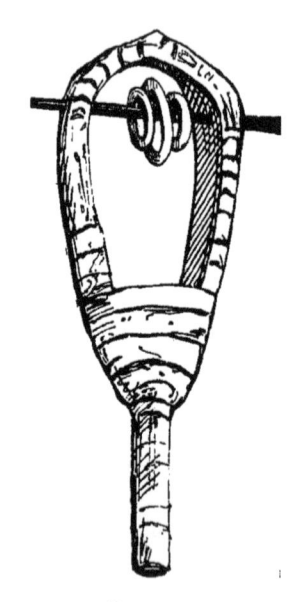

Sistrim

Sistrims are percussion instruments much like a tambourine. It had a U-shaped metal frame, made of wood, or bronze with several wires strung across it. Bells or small rings of metal were placed on these to produce a sound ranging from a tinkling to a loud metallic crash. They could be used as a sound effect at a suitable part of the music or shaken as a rhythmic instrument. It was a sacred instrument in

---

[10] Anyone who has seen me dance would be hard pressed to spot the difference, but since I don't particularly like night clubs the trance state does tend to help me leave and go somewhere interesting while at the same time participating in what is considered an important part of British culture.

ancient Egypt, particularly in the worship of the goddess Hathor, because its shape looked like a cow. It was used to scare off bad spirits and became later associated with the Cat Goddess Bast.

I have used one as an alternative to a drum with great success. It is a great ritual tool with to open sacred space.

Other instruments

We know the Ancient Egyptians used many different percussion instruments. There were clappers, some of which were made in the shape of human hands and cymbals. Less familiar to modern musicians were the Crotal which were two small cymbals on the ends of joined wooden clappers. There was also a menit, which was a shaker made of strands of beads. All these can be used by someone hoping to recreate a pre-dynastic Egyptian shaman's armoury.

Making instruments magical

As I said in my book 'Making Talismans', a Siberian shaman's musical instruments were considered too magically powerful ordinary people. After his or her death, they were treated like toxic waste and taken away from people in case they caused them magical harm.

Obviously magical tools do not get this way simply by playing them and throwing them into a cupboard afterwards. They must be like a part of you. To do that, you have to make as many links to the instrument and yourself as possible.

Ideally, you should hunt the animal that will provide the skin for your drum. You should kill it, cut the skin from it, hang it on a sacred tree, when it dried, the decayed flesh is scrapped off, it is soaked in acid and urine to remove any hair and then clean it. You should cut down a tree hollow it out and tie the skins to it and tighten it over the edge. Then, cause the skin to shrink tighter over the drum with a sacred flame.

Obviously there are few that can do this. You might be able to hunt a stray dog or two in the local park, but you are going to find yourself up on an animal cruelty charge if you kill it. Besides since most modern shamans consider it better to remain at one with all life it is no longer considered politically correct to go round killing it.

Instead it is better to pop around the shops and buy one. You can then personalise it in any way you like. Painting is the best method. I have seen some marvellous drums lovingly painted with Egyptian Gods and hieroglyphs that were special to the shamans that used them. You should be careful the paint you use on the skins of any drums does not cause them to shrink or warp. It is best to use acrylic paint to do this. If you can wait for the paint to dry, and you do not apply the paint too thickly it will cope with being walloped for a long time before it starts to flake off. You might like to paint the drum in colours you like. Most African drums you buy come in a natural wood, but there is no reason yours cannot be covered from head to toe with illustrations from the Book of the Dead.

Somewhere you should put your name on it. This should be transcribed in hieroglyphs as we describe in chapter four. This will help form the magical link between you and the instrument. This applies to all the musical instruments and magical items you use. It is possible to carve these hieroglyphs or paint them onto the item.

To make these even more magical it is important to set them aside still further with a consecration ritual. This is based on a later Egyptian ritual called the 'Opening of the Mouth'. This rite has obvious shamanic overtones and was used until the collapse of Roman Egypt. One of the first references we have to it is in the Old Kingdom Pyramid texts. The rite was performed by the Sem priest, who we have mentioned earlier was a relative of the pre-dynastic shamans. The rite was performed to enable the mummy to communicate to the priests. A much later collection of magical and mystical Egyptian works called the Hermetica, describes how statues were ensouled and filled with spirit. Priests used the ritual of the opening of the mouth on objects to allow the spirits to talk through them.

Again we have no proof of this in the pre-dynastic period, but rite does fit the job well. This ceremony was painted on a tomb-chapel in Rekhmira in 1425 BC. It provided me with a ritual from which

I could write this much simplified version. Where the ritual seems rougher or stranger it is when I have used the translated words of the original ceremony. I have also used the original Egyptian names of the Gods rather than their more familiar Greek counterparts.

The goal of the ritual is to find and give your instrument a spirit, which will empower your workings and give you a guide. You meet the spirit of the drum, name it, ask it to become the drum and speak through it.

To perform the ceremony you will need some sand, a sharp rock, and an iron axe head. You should also have a small stick that looks like it could be a snake and four small cups of water, a bowl of rock salt, a stick of incense and a bottle of wine. You should sit in the centre of the sacred space with the items available. Ideally the rite should be outdoors. It will take some time and should not be rushed. If you want to do it properly you can go and camp in the wilderness and take a night to do the ritual. It would be good if you could perform the rite near a river as this would be a link to the sacred Nile.

Preparation

You should prepare yourself by creating sacred space as was described in the previous chapter. And sitting in the space with your drum meditating on what it means. You should see it as a person, as a guide, or friend and you should have a name for it. Picture yourself talking to it, but you should not play it yet. Cast the sand onto the floor and place the instrument with its top facing the south. Put the four cups of water in the East, South, North and West of the drum.

The Rite

Take the glass of water from the East and walk around the instrument flicking water at it.

Chanting the name Hor[11] Take the Water from the South and repeat the previous action. This time you should chant the name Set.

Repeat the same process in the west and the North chanting the

---

[11] Horus or Heru

name Djehuty[12] in the west and Dunanwy in the North
Stand in the East, face East and say *"pure, pure, pure, pure for <insert the name of the drum>"*

> Pause and say: *"I have fastened for you your head to your bones before Geb. Djehuty purifies you."*

Pause. Take the salt and walk around the drum four times flicking the salt at it. Stand in the east and face east and say

> *"Pure, pure, pure, pure <name of the drum>*
> *Natron for your mouth to be open*
> *Oh <name of the drum> May you taste its taste in front of the divine pavilion*
> *Natron[13] is in the mouth of Hor and Seth*
> *Natron is the heart of Hor and Seth*
> *Your mouth is washed with the purification of the gods and the followers of Hor*

Take the rock
Walk around the instrument four times saying each time you go around

> *Pure, pure, for <name of instrument>*
> *You are washed, Hor is washed, you are washed, Set is washed,*
> *You are washed, Djehuty is washed, you are washed, Dunanwy is washed,*
> *You are washed and balanced between them*
> *Your mouth is the mouth of a milk calf,*
> *You are in the lap of your mother Iset*

Light the incense and walk around the instrument four times saying each time

> *You are censed, Hor is censed, you are censed, Seth is censed*

---

[12] Thoth

[13] A type of salt. In this book we mix salt with bicarbonate of soda to get a similar effect.

You are censed, Djehuty is censed, you are censed, Dunanwy is censed
Your Spirit is censed, you are censed, you are censed,
You are censed, a bridge between your brothers the gods,
Your head is censed, your speech is censed and you are purified

Sit down and cover yourself in your blanket. Picture yourself standing beside the Nile. Imagine the drum as a human or an animal coming towards you. Do not rush this. It will take some time.

After you have contacted the spirit of the drum you must ask it to indwell into the body you have created for it. If it doesn't want to, then you will have to get another instrument! Sometimes it is not the right time for you to own such an ensouled instrument. You should return and end the ceremony down immediately.

Trying to be aware of both your visualisation and your physical reality, you kiss the drum and say:

"I have come as your embracer, I am Hor
I have pressed your mouth for you, I am your son whom you love"

Take the rock and draw the outline of the spirit of the drum which you saw around it. Say:

I am Hor and Seth
I shall protect you.

Put down the drum and walk around it four times pouring the wine onto the ground as you do so.

By this sacrifice are the two lands of above and below joined.

Hold the drum in your arms. You should see yourself as Aset raising life from the dead.

Imagine the form of drum spirit merge with the body of the drum. Take the stone and tap it again four times on the skin and then four times where you see the spirit's eyes.

Say: <Name of the drum>   I have pressed your mouth for you. I have opened your mouth for you. I have balanced your mouth and *bones for you.*

Then take the snake shaped stick. Tap the drum skin four times and then four times where you see the spirit's eyes.

Say: <name of the drum> I have opened your mouth for you with the foreleg of life.

Now picture a starry night. See the stars form into a Goddess. She stands over the drum and wraps herself around the spirit and the drum.

Say:

Newet has been raised over you,
She has brought you all gods
You have come into being in your strength,
You have come into being as the sustenance of all gods,
Oh Anhur[14], Shu son of Tem[15], they speak to <name of instrument>,
as he or she lives, they live
May Shu protection the life of <name of instrument>
Oh this <name of instrument> Hor has opened your mouth for you,
he opens your eyes for you
With the double-god blade, with the Great-of-Power blade, with which the mouth of every god is opened

Take the axe head and tap the instrument on the skin with it four times

<Name of the instrument> your mouth is opened. I have balanced your mouth and bones for you
<Name of the instrument> I have opened your mouth for you
<Name of the instrument> I open your mouth for you with the nua-blade
I have opened your mouth for you with the nua-blade,
The meskhetyu-blade of iron, that opens the mouths of the gods
May <name of the instrument> walk and speak with his body

---

[14] Ausar or Osiris
[15] A form of Atum

before the great Nine Gods in the great mansion of the official that is in Iunu

Draw the eye of Hor upon the drum with left over wine and say:

Receive the eye of Hor, your face is not deprived of it
Receive the eye of Hor it cannot fly away
Pour the four glasses of water onto the ground by the drum
Receive the eye of Hor; the water in it is purity for you

Holding the drum towards the East say:
"I dedicate <name of drum> to the spirits of light
And declare that <his or her> mouth is opened to guide me as I sail the boat of millions of years into the Underworld and the heavens. And when my time on earth is done and I enter the Judgment Hall of Maat, may it too pass to the lands of the West.

Now you may use the instrument. However it should be covered when not in use and you should not allow another to play it unless you have permission from the spirit itself.

Chapter Four

Animal Totems

Pre-dynastic Egyptians had a much closer relationship with animals and their ancestors. This changed under the reigns of the Pharaohs of the Old and Middle Kingdoms, but enough vestiges remain for us to make a stab at what our early shaman's were doing.

In the Native American tradition animal spirits were guides from the Great Spirit. A person would 'cry for a vision' of their animal guide in a special rite and if one showed up it often became a lifetime or temporary guide or totem animal for them. Modern shamans have taken this idea and called the animals that teach us something power animals or guides. Power animals or Guides that represent our work in this lifetime are more important and are called Totem animals. Totem animals have been our guides and teachers for many lifetimes. They sound a lot like what in psychology is our Higher or Overself. However, just as an animal has its limits over the human, the Totem animal falls short as an expression of the total that our Higher Self represents. The Totem animal is closer to the idea of what we call in Hermetic Magic, the Holy Guardian Angel. This is part of the Higher Self which makes sure that we live our destinies and protect us from the results of our failings.

There is a belief among modern shamans that people from the same Totem have karmic links that go back through many lifetimes.

Each region of Egypt, or Nome, focused on the worship of a single animal deity or what modern shamans call Totem animals. This does not mean that some people did not have individual animals assigned to them. Some individuals somehow selected their own and were named after them -- thus we have the Scorpion King, the Lion King and the Elephant King. Other rulers took the names of Gods, who were then   animals and birds.

But why would they have used animals and what would these have meant to them? Pre-dynastic Egypt was no longer a hunter-gatherer based culture. Animals were not as important to the people as food, so there can only been one explanation -- each animal was symbolic. What the creature or plant decided the symbol's nature. The hawk, for example, flies high the sky. It sits still in the air, hovering almost still waiting to see movement from high up. It is not surprising that it became associated with the Sun. The Scorpion sting results in death by suffocation, it is resistant to hunger and thirst, and hid in the mud-bricks of Egyptian houses. It became associated with war and protection.

When we face animal powers in our vision quests or meditations, they are a symbolic key to a part of the universe. They are not 'animals', but ideas that come from the part of the universe the animal spirits have mastered. As a result they become disembodied teachers by being themselves. One of the problems I have with modern shamanic techniques is they stress that you should have an affinity with any totem animal you work with. Many modern shamans miss the point, believing that it should be an animal they like. As a result there are profusion of people who claim they have dog and cat totems (or their extensions Lion and Wolf) but few wildebeest, aardvarks, or vultures. We want our power animals to be, a bit anthropomorphic, and to teach us that everything will be alright. The reverse is true. You get a much more primal idea of what the animal represents from one of the less domesticated animals to whom we have not had a chance to anthropomorphise into something more human..

I did a shamanic circle once with a strict vegan dog lover. Not surprisingly, she was convinced that 'dog' was her totem animal. There was nothing 'dog like' about her, she was independent and a person who could tell you the toxins in your cup of coffee to three decimal places. She often was happy just go off into the mountains, by herself, to be with nature.

A group of us performed a shamanic working to go to the land of our totem animal and learn something from them. The person in charge of the working made a mistake and told us to call our totem animal and assumed that everyone knew what their animal was.

In the post-journey cup of tea afterwards, I noticed that Sue was looking a bit white and I asked her what was wrong. It turned out that in her vision quest Dog had shown up with a pack of his mates and together they bought down a small faun. The pack then tore the little body apart, fought over the scraps and then trotted down and crawled over one another and fell asleep[1].

When I look at the list of animal totems the Egyptians used, I don't see much in the way of animals that will be that kind to would-be shamans either. The cat untamed in our period, although the dog was. Any Egyptian cat spirit will be closer to the primal vicious, furry ball of small knives it had been for millions of years. The people of the Nile built doors to keep them out and would never have dreamed of installing a cat flap.

Shamans used animals in much the same way as later Egyptian priests used Gods. There would be the Totem animal of the Region (or Nome), then there would be a totem for the village which most people would share. There is scant evidence for people having personal totems, however some women had tattoos with figures of animals. Shamans, however, used the powers of the many different totem animals to work their magic. In the last chapter we looked at the idea of assuming godforms as the method of focusing magical power. If a shaman wanted to cure a warrior of fear, he might go into a trance, contact the Lion power animal, assume it, come back to the person he was seeking to cure [2] and pour that energy into them. The Shaman could project the godform of the Lion onto the aura of the patent, perhaps changing their name to Lion afterwards.

Native North American Indians talk about how people could 'cry for a vision' of a power animal to advise them in a time of need.

---

[1] With my typical tact, I said "oh my god, you killed Bambi." She looked at me and said "It's not funny, OK!!"
[2] If they hadn't run away.

Sometimes these visions are physical creatures, such as birds or animals stumbling around the vision questor's hut, or they were dream teachers who spoke words.

Below is a list of Totem or 'power' animals that we know lived in pre-dynastic Egypt and some of their potential meanings. These are based on some of my own experiences and the list is not exhaustive. You will notice that I have given their names in Ancient Egyptian. These can act like magical words of power which you can chant when you want to contact your animal totem. As part of the seeking, they will give you their name, this will be specific to you and will be more powerful. You should write these names down and never tell anyone what they are:

Anteater: The Anteater might be the Set beast which has confused Egyptologists for centuries. To understand why you have to understand to the Egyptians order was important. To them the ant, must have been a role model of that divine order. Set, who was originally the God of the Desert, represented those wild storms that upset their divine order. Anyone who has seen an anteater attack a nest of ants will know that it destroys the order that is inherent in the burrow. Anteater can teach how to break down structures that are outworn, how to remove that in our lives that forces us into a narrow existence.

Baboon: The dog-headed baboon was the most intelligent of animals and became linked to Tehuti, the god of writing, which is cerebral. Hedjwer, or the Great White One was a baboon god, who may have had a connection with the ancestors (which is a good idea connected to the theory of evolution). Another baboon symbol became God Babi (bull of the baboons). He represented male dominance and power. Egyptians called him in spells of violence and fear. Anyone who has seen male baboon's fighting will understand this symbol of our primitive and violent selves and understand it has much to teach us.

Beetle: The Egyptians paid much attention to the scarab, or dung beetle. The Scarab rolls a ball of dung across the ground as a takeaway meals-on-wheels for its lava to live in. The dung beetle buried the dung and the eggs in the sand. When these eggs hatched, the dung beetles emerged from the earth making it a symbol of instant creation. In this role the scarab became the God of the sunrise Khepri. They equated the dung ball with the sun as Re rolled it across the sky. The scarab teaches the lessons of death and rebirth and how life comes into being. The totem shows how to gain and then let go so a new life may emerge.

Cat: During our period, cats were pests. There were four types of cat in pre-dynastic Egypt, excluding the big cats which get their own category. All these different cats can teach skills. All these totems are protective, they can teach 'hunting' in its widest sense; observation, listening, patience and stealth.

- The African Wildcat, which is large, yellow-gray, and eats small game. It looks like a domestic cat, but has longer legs and tail. It is often brown with a stripe down the back. This breed became tame during the Middle Kingdom. It hunts small prey.

- The Swamp Cat, which looks like a large domestic cat with a short tail and tufted ears. They have acute sight and hearing, good scent and hunt small mammals, birds, reptiles, including snakes, fish and eggs. They are usually nocturnal and live in cliffs and caves.

- The Sand Cat, are small short legged cats with fox-like faces. They live in burrows and eat desert mammals such as mice, birds and reptiles. They have good eye sight and have large territories.

- Caracal are large nocturnal cats with tufted ears. They are famous for their bird hunting skills and famous for their bird hunting skills, and can grab a bird from the air with a high leap. Have excellent sight and hearing, and good sense of smell. They live in caves and on cliffs.

Cow: During our period the Goddess Het-Hor and Nut were cows. The cow was the driving force behind Egyptian agriculture and linked to female fertility. During our period they were the long-horned variety. It can teach insight, focused thought and developing a nurturing spirit.

Cobra: There were three goddesses connected to the cobra. There was Wadjet, who represented Lower Egypt and kingship. The cobra goddess Renenet was a fertility goddess who was a nurse and protector. There was Meretseger, 'she who loves silence', who bought justice to criminals. The Cobra totem teaches decisive and sudden actions. It has the ability to hypnotize its pray and how to hide oneself until the right moment.

Crocodile: Crocodiles and hippopotamuses have dual positive and negative meanings. On one hand they are the forces of evil that impede your life path, yet on the other the have their positive uses. Ammut, was a demoness at the judgment hall of the dead who punished evildoers by eating their hearts. Sobek, who was portrayed as a human with the head of a crocodile, or as the crocodile itself and was a great protective deity. Crocodile is a creature that can show us how to walk between worlds, how to hide ourselves. It can teach about maternal power, revenge, aggression and primitive survival instincts.

Dog: Wild dogs were tamed during our period and are therefore a good connection between the wild world of Nature and our own. One breed that we know about was similar to the Saluki breed. They can act as loyal guides to the more primal regions of the spiritual world. It is important to distinguish between such dogs, which are made the way they are by humanity, and wild dogs. Both show up in vision quests.

Elephant: The North African elephant was smaller than the Asian (Indian) or Bush variety and measures about 2.35 meters at the shoulder. The Egyptians did not tame the African elephant until the Greeks annexed Egypt. They were extinct by the second century BC after centuries of hunting. Egyptians believed the elephant had no joints in its legs and slept standing up. They were religious and worshipped the moon and stars. Elephants can teach wisdom and patience.

Falcon: Connected with the Gods Re and Hor, the falcon was a bird that had protective powers and the sun. The falcon was linked to Montu, god of war, and Sokar the god of the dead. Falcon teaches patience and the capacity to see what is going on rather than illusion. They are protectors but they have the ability to see into the future and predict where a life pattern is leading.

Frog: There were many gods connected to frog imagery. The Egyptians connected them with fertility, childbirth, and resurrection. Frog teaches the ability to transform and evolve and jump out of any ruts.

Goose: The goose was the sacred animal of Geb, who was the earth god. Because of the Goose association he was known as 'The Great Cackler'. Geese were the original guard dogs and were seen as protectors. Goose teaches beauty, tradition, how to receive, they are connected ritual and sociality.

Heron: The heron was an important totem animal and much of its myth was gained by the phoenix. The heron was a bird of the sun and rebirth. It was associated with the flood of the Nile and of the creation. As this is that it is seen as standing alone on isolated rocks of islands of high ground during the floods, just like life which rose from the watery chaos at the first creation.

Hare: The Hare is considered a creature of great madness and freedom. The animal was later connected to Ausar who was sometimes called Wepuat or Un-nefer and portrayed with a hare's head. A hare was sacrificed to the Nile each year to guarantee the annual flood. There was a goddess called Unut or Wenet and she was depicted with the head of a Hare too. The Hare was a messenger of the God Tehuti (Wisdom and Magic) so a harebrained scheme to the Ancient Egyptians was a cunning plan. In art the hare was shown greeting the dawn symbolised the essence of life itself. The Hare totem is a guide between us and the gods, it teaches sacrifice and liberation.

Hippopotamus: To the ancient Egyptians, the hippopotamus was one of the most dangerous animals many of them would face. They were a hazard for small fishing boats and other rivercraft which were the main way of travelling and living off the Nile. It is not surprising then the male hippopotamus was considered an evil animal. Like the crocodile, a hippopotamus is a sign of the forces that oppose us on our path. They move in our subconscious mind and can threaten to sink us. The female hippopotamus was seen as Taweret, the caring hippo goddess of fertility and childbirth. She would protect pregnant mothers during childbirth. It might have been that she only did this only if she was placated by her worshippers. A would-be Shaman meeting hippopotamuses should be careful. They can show you deeper aspects of your unconscious mind, but these can turn around and sink you.

Ibis: This bird was later linked to the God of magic and writing, Tehuti. One reason for this is their cry is a bit like 'aha', which had the same meaning to the Ancient Egyptians. There were three types of Ibis, the sacred ibis, the hermit ibis and the glossy ibis. The one we are most interested in is the Sacred Ibis, which lives in marshes and has is mostly white with a black head and neck and some black plumes in the tail. It has a long, slender, down-curved, black bill. The legs are long with partially webbed feet. Not only does it teach us how to understand the problems that face us, it was thought the Ibis protected Egypt from plagues and serpents.

Jackal: The jackal was associated with Anu, the god of the dead and with Wepwawet, the Opener of the Ways, who performed the Opening of the Mouth ceremony. The jackal was thought to be a guide to the newly dead because they were often seen around the desert and mountains where the tombs were built. They lived in holes in the ground and so were connected to the Underworld. This is one of the most important totem animals for Shamans, even if it is not your own one. They can teach much about death and the experience of walking between the worlds. Although in later Egyptian art the jackal was always black, Egyptian jackals are brown.

Lions: Lions are associated with leadership and bravery. It was a test of a Pre-dynastic ruler to hunt and kill a Lion. Therefore, there were few wild lions by the Pharonic period. Lions usually lived on the edges of the desert, and were the guardians of the eastern and western horizons, where Re rose and set. The Lion-god, Aker guarded the gateway to the netherworld. Lion paw motifs were used to symbolise protection on beds. The Lion represented a force that could be dangerous if it got out of control. The stories of the later lioness goddess Sekhmet, who killed evil but did not care about "friendly fire" is a case in point.

Lepidotus fish: Fish were unclean and were not eaten. In fact in some rituals they were ceremonially hauled out of the Nile to be trodden underfoot, in a general attack on Set who was considered to be behind the whole fishy thing. The main reason was when Ausar had been cut up and parts of his body distributed to different parts of Egypt, a fish ate his penis. This meant that when Ausar was rebuilt by his wife, she was unable to compete the job and had to build a golden penis. However there is some evidence the Lepidotus fish was worshipped under the Goddess Hat-mehit. As the cult of Ausar grew and the legend about the fish expanded. Her influence was reduced when she got a husband, the Ram god BaNebDjede. Fish teaches about movement and change and how to work with your unconscious mind to deal with your deepest fears and hopes.

Oryx: The Oryx was an emblem of Set, the God of deserts and storms. This was a strange attribution, as we have said earlier Set was not renown for his organisation and Oryx are subject to a hierarchical organisation within the herd. However since Set ruled over many desert animals, and the Oryx could be seen eating plants that could kill a human, perhaps this attribution is not surprising. Later depictions show Heru riding an oryx which show the Oryx was seen as a more tamable aspect of the shadow, a bit like a bad habit that you are just about to master. In fact during the Old Kingdom period they even tried to tame these animals with some degree of success. The Oryx teaches how to adapt those parts of our lives that would normally cripple us and make them useful. It shows us that our dark side can be useful.

Ostrich: This bird was hunted for its meat and eggs from early times. It was a symbol of divine law and order and the Goddess Maat. Symbolically it is an important totem animal because it is a bird which cannot fly. In other words it had a chose of flying with the spirits, but has, like humanity chosen to gain its experience by walking the earth. It does this quickly as it can run at speeds of up to 40 miles an hour. It is a huge bird that can yet camouflage itself by lying on the ground. The Ostrich teaches us how to live our lives practically and set rules for ourselves that are based on truth. It shows how we can be individuals within this framework, even if we blend in.

Omormyrus fish: There was one exception to fish prejudice, the Omormyrus fish was considered to have been created out of the god's wounds. It was connected to Het-Hor and accompanied the solar barque as an advanced scout and wanted of any attacks by Apep. As a Totem animal it is a way shower. It shows a way through trials and suffering. It helps heal psychological scars.

Pig: Pigs were herded, raised, and eaten by poorer people, throughout our period. Connected with the God Set, who during pre-dynastic times was not considered a bad guy they were associated with grubbing in the dirt and eating rubbish. So, they weren't eaten that much or regarded that fondly. Parts of pig's bodies were used to cure illnesses ranging from cancer to blindness. The Pig Totem can help you to root out the answers to problems. They are especially good at teaching clairsentience and clairaudience.

Scorpion: The Scorpion was an important pre-dynastic totem. People were terrified of the sting and believed that by placating scorpion gods, they would leave you alone. They hunt alone and prefer hot dry places. They can teach people how to defend themselves in life, how to search for an opponent's weak spots, and then strike effectively. They are good teachers on the subject of neurotic control and jealousy.

Sheep: Sheep were kept for their meat, milk, skins and wool. Rams were fertility symbols and identified with various gods, notably Khnum, a creator god, and Amun. As a Totem sheep have a connection with creating the building blocks of life. It can teach about working in groups and building societies and material power.

Snake: The Snake was an important symbol in early times. It was mostly because people were terrified by them. We have already looked at the Cobra totem. Other snakes in Egypt where not seen in such a positive light. The supreme bad guy of the Egyptian pantheon in any time was the snake demon Apep. Apep, was the chaos that rivalled the Egyptian Maat. At night Apep would take on to stop Re has he entered the underworld. If he ever succeeded, the sun would not rise and Chaos would rule the earth. Other snakes included Naunet (water), Amaunet (invisibility), Hauhet (infinity) and Kauket (darkness). As a totem Snake teaches how to deal with fear, how to strip away those things that are dead within us, or old habits and be reborn. It can show how to see into the hearts of people. They can be guides into the otherworld.

Turtle: The Turtle was considered a bad being by the ancient Egyptians because, like Apep, he tried to stop the Sun rising. He was associated with night, darkness and evil. During our period it was allowed to eat Turtles, but later it became an abomination. It is possible the turtle was even considered a scapegoat and where the sins of the people were whispered to it before it was ceremonially killed. As a totem it teaches of the darkness of the subconscious, how to build armour and protection, about the need to walk between worlds. They also teach how to pattern one's life to spend the maximum time on earth.

Vulture: There were five different species of vulture lived in ancient Egypt, although the one seen in the hieroglyph was the 'griffon' vulture. Egyptians thought it important because it was a great recycler and eating of dead flesh. The vulture associated with the goddess Nekhebet who was the benefactor of the city of El-Kab in Upper Egypt. When El-Kab became important early in ancient Egyptian history, the vulture soon became a heraldic creature for all of Upper Egypt. Vultures were seen as great mothers. The Vulture totem can teach people how to be Resourceful, patient and focused on their goal. They will show you how to clean up a mess and free things from the old that are needed in the new.

Totem Trees and plants

Some areas didn't have totem animals, but might have had power trees. Although in later periods we know that some gods had trees that were sacred to them, there were a series of trees that had a significance which might have been a remnant of a form of tree worship.

Where it exists, tree worship follows an earlier religious belief that a natural object has its spirit. It is important to honour or give respect to these spirits and their destruction was terrible. Such cultures will not cut a tree except under special ritualistic circumstances and will only use fallen branches. Other cultures think that only some trees are special. In Africa silk-cotton trees, which have enormous trunks were worshipped simply because of their size. Other cases the souls of the Gods or the dead use the tree as a body when they live on earth. This is closer to what the Ancient Egyptians had in mind. . In the myth of Ausar, the god was enclosed in the trunk of a tamarisk tree, which was later cut down and used as a pillar in the palace of the King of Byblos. Although he was a Corn God, Ausar's symbol for a longtime was the tamarisk tree trunk, was called Djed. Over time the tree trunk was replaced by the imagery of a pillar which became known as the Djed Pillar, the Pillar of Stability.

This legend suggests an earlier form of worship where a God indwells in a sacred tree, rather than the tree itself being special.

It would be tempting to think the south and northern Sycamores had a magical totem tree of this species. However, the Egyptians thought that twin sycamores stood at the eastern gate of heaven from which the sun god Re emerged each morning. The sycamore was connected to Het-Hor, who was given the epithet Lady of the Sycamore. It is more likely then the statue of Het-Hor was placed in a special Sycamore tree to be worshipped .

Important trees and plants were:

Acacia: Sacred to Hor. In mythology, the gods were born under the acacia tree of the goddess Saosis who was another version of Het-Hor. Part of the Boat of Re was made from Acacia wood.

Blue Lotus: The Egyptian Lotus was a water lily. It was closely connected to the sun because it opens in the morning at sunrise and closes at sunset. Nefertem, the God of Perfume and healing was associated with this flower. It has been suggested the pre-dynastic shamans and the later priests may have extracted some form of narcotic from the Lotus. It appears the flowers contain a substance called nuciferine. This is not normally seen as psychoactive but when the flowers are soaked in alcohol for a few days it had an effect like a mild form of LSD.

Persea: This is a fruit-bearing deciduous tree which is likely to be the tree which the Egyptians called ished. This was a magical tree on which Tehuti wrote the name of the kings at coronation and jubilee festivals. This was a divine promise their lives would be perpetuated.

Tamarisk tree: The Tamarisk Tree was an important part of the Ausar myth. It was sacred to Wepwawet, who was the conductor of the souls of the dead and related to the Jackal totem animal. In a side issue in Genesis 21:33 it states that Abraham planted a tamarisk tree in Beersheba, and called there on the name of Yahweh, the Everlasting God. In the Book of the Dead utterance 574 the dead person says to the Tamarisk Tree:

> *"Hail to thee tree which encloses the god, under which the gods of the Lower Sky stand, the end of which is cooked, the inside of which is burnt, which sends out the pains of death: may you gather those who are in the Abyss, may you assemble those who are in the celestial expanses."*

There is nothing recorded as to what the tree said back.

Sycamore: The Sycamore was sacred to Re. It was regarded as an expression of Het-Hor and later goddesses Nut, Aset, and especially of Het-Hor, who was given the epithet Lady of the Sycamore. Sycamores were often planted near tombs, and burial in coffins

Animal Totems

made of sycamore wood returned the dead person to the womb of the mother tree goddess

Willow: Sacred to Ausar. It was said that when he lay in his coffin, Willow trees grew up to protect him. Towns in Egypt, that were associated with Ausar, often had sacred groves of Willow trees.

Totem objects

There are some symbols that appear on various hieroglyphs that could be totem objects. The first was the phallus which was associated with the worship of Amsu, Geb and Amon. It could be that phallic worship was more common in an earlier period and that many of the 'phallic objects' that find their way in Egyptian ritual may have been vestiges of a more overt worship.

Our Egyptian shaman would be familiar with these animals and the various powers they offered. For reasons we will look at in the next chapter, he would be familiar with the Nomes that each of these totems would have ruled.

Totems of Upper and Lower Egypt

Upper Egypt

1.	Ta-Sety	Crocodile
2.	Throne of Heru	Hawk
3.	Shrine	Vulture
4.	Sceptre	Sheep
5.	Two Falcons	Falcon
6.	Crocodile	Crocodile
7.	Sistrum	Cow
8.	Great Land	Ausar
9.	Amsu	Phallus
10.	Cobra	Cobra
11.	Set	Ant eater
12.	Viper	Snake
13.	Upper pomegranate	Jackel

14.	Lower pomegranate	Cow
15.	Hare	Hare
16.	Oryx	Oryx
17.	Jackel	Jackel
18.	Anti	Falcon
19.	Two Sceptres	Mormyrus fish
20.	South Sycamore	Cow
21.	Northern Sycamore	Cow
22.	Knife	Crocodile

Lower Egypt

1	White Wall	Hawk
1.	Foreleg	Cow
2.	West	Hawk/Ostrich
3.	Southern Shield	Lotus/Crocodile
4.	Northern Shield	Ausar
5.	Mountain Bull	Bull
6.	Western Harpoon	Snake
7.	Eastern Harpoon	Sheep
8.	Andjety	Ausar
9.	Black Ox	Cow
10.	Ox-Count	Cow
11.	Calf and Cow	Cow
12.	Prospering Sceptre	Sheep
13.	Foremost of the East	Anteater
14.	Ibis	Ibis
15.	Fish	Lepidotus fish
16.	Behdet	Hawk
17.	Prince of the South	Cat
18.	Prince of the North	Cobra

Some of these names are much later than our period. For example the two Nomes named pomegranate must have either been later divisions, or had earlier names. This is because the pomegranate was introduced into Egypt in the Middle Kingdom. In cases were the

Animal Totems

name or the Cartouche of the Nome fails to give a clue what the Totem might have been, I have assigned one based on the Gods or Goddesses that were worshipped in that area. This is unreliable as some of the areas that have obvious animal totems have gods which would have generated different totem using this method.

You will notice there are two exceptions to assigning animals to each Nome. The first is the worship of Ausar as a Totem from an early period and the other is the strange case of Southern Shield where the Lotus was used but so was the worship of Sobek.

Finding a personal totem

It is unlikely that ordinary Egyptian people had a personal totem. They considered themselves so linked to their tribe, Nome or chieftain they considered their personal religious quest as their s. In modern times this is unacceptable. Ordinary people, whose contribution is just as important as any politicians or kings walk this path. The purpose of working any magic is to find and identify our own Higher Self and to do that we need some form of guides.

It is important to identify what these guides are. The American Indians say that in their purest form, animal guides or Totems are specialised forms of the One God. This might be true. However the person seeing or experiencing those guides sees them through the magic mirror of their own unconscious mind. This always colours the view to the point the experience is so heavily garnished that it could be a different dish.

A person who has been bitten by a dog and is frightened of them is unlikely to find that animal as a guide. However that does not mean their totem animal is not a dog, usually they will colour their vision until they find an animal that is similar characteristics like a seal. The evil dog will still show up as a messenger of evil. These totems will not tell you something that you do not know. This is because the energy can only communicate with what it finds in your subconscious mind. If you have never been taught how to speak Bulgarian, no inner world creature can teach you. But your unconscious contains all the memories and information that you have seen and heard since you first crawled out of the womb. So if you wanted to learn Bulgarian and had a few lessons and lived with a Bulgarian, an inner guide will be able to help you.

Animal guides are rarely going to talk to you, instead you will learn by seeing or doing it with them in your inner reality. You will then have to come back and think about your experience so it makes sense.

An animal guide will tell you want you need to know, not what you think you need to know. This is because their nature is a lot more primal and they work closer with needs and drives rather than intellectual information.

Some modern magicians, such as RJ Stewart, will argue that an understanding of psychology kills off shamanic techniques. They argue, with some justification, that intellectualising the experience, or trying to understand it with the mind, is a pointless exercise. However, ancient mystery traditions never accepted a seer channelled as gospel truth. The priesthood meditated on the message until they understood its full symbolic meaning. A working knowledge of how the mind works helps us to rule out those experiences that are essentially our own egos talking to us.

It is vital if we have an animal guide that is insisting that we should go and set up a new religion with us as the new messiah that we ditch it rather than listen to it. Guides that insist on being worshipped, or tell us that we are worthless should be sent packing. These are all extensions of our own subconscious mind. They might have been stirred by higher spirits, but the message has become so clouded they are useless for us.

We need to know when we meet a being or a scenario on the inner planes that it is not something the shrinks call 'wish fulfilment'. This happens when we want something so much that we make it happen on the inner planes.

Ancient shamans knew this, although they did not use psychological terminology. There is an interesting case in the book 'Holographic Universe' where the author describes his experience with some believable beings who claimed to have created the universe. When he described the experience to the Shaman who was helping him to experience the vision, he was told these beings were tricksters and the clue was that "They always claim to say they created everything."

A shaman needs to find a Totem. If you meet an animal that is not on the list, you should check to see if it ever existed in Ancient Egypt. You can do that by checking it up on the Internet or at the local library. If it doesn't appear, see if there is an equivalent. For example if you got an Indian elephant, it is likely to be an African elephant. It might take imagination, but it is possible.

There might be some people who are on the shamanic path and might have already worked out what their totem animal is, who are wondering what the advantage is of adapting their totem animal to an equivalent Egyptian one. What we are trying to do is build a symbolic alphabet here. It will not work if we have a badger or a skunk leading us through the Egyptian underworld, the Gods would look at you strangely and point.

Ceremony of Finding

Prepare your sacred space. If you have a drum you might like to play it, if not, curl in the position of the sleeping shaman.

In your mind's eye enter the inner shaman's hut, meditate on the fire for a few minutes and then wrap yourself in your blanket. See yourself as stepping out of your body, as if you were a ghost, walk out of the hut and towards the river. It is night and the protective gate around the village is shut, but you pass through the walls as if they were not there. You come down to riverbank. There is a reed boat there. You get into the boat.

As if by magic it drifts across the darkened river. You arrive at the other side and get out of the boat. You are standing on the western side of the river. This is the land of the Shaman, for it is the side of the river where the dead are buried. You walk towards the west.

After a while you come to some rough desert hills. You climb these slowly. You come to a ridge. Looking down you see the Nile snaking towards the sea. Behind you is the desert.

Still within your vision stand with your arms outstretched and say:

"I send my voice from the Western to the Eastern Horizon, in the land of Khem, over which Re sails his boat.
I call about the two lands and ask the Gods for the gift of my Totem animal
My link the past and the Future, that speaks to my High Soul.
I ask for this that I may serve the land and the Gods."

Now you wait, trying to hold your vision as long as possible. Watch over the land. You might see many animals or birds or see a fish in the river below, however they must approach you and make some sign that you must follow them.

If nothing happens, and you attention wanders, you should picture yourself going back to your village and try again on another day.

If a being approaches or calls, you should approach it and ask it:

"Have you been appointed by the Gods as my Totem animal?"

If it points out that it has, you should ask it its name. It will find a way of making this clear to you. It might be letter by letter, or simply an image in your mind. You should then thank it and return to your village, and back into this time and this reality.

You should then study everything you can about this animal, its Egyptian habitat, and how it lives. This will help you understand what will happen to you later.

❊ ❊ ❊

Now it is time to integrate the Totem animal into you inner reality.

In your next spirit vision you should imagine yourself sitting outside your hut. You will have a thick pole of timber about seven foot tall that you are carving.

Imagine yourself chiselling the animal, bird, or fish on the top of the pole. Imagine it as carefully as you can.

Then when it is finished paint it in a proper colour.

While the paint dries, meditate on what the animal totem means to you intellectually.

Then dig a hole in the ground before your hut and with the help of the villagers raise the totem upwards. Set a few rocks into the ground so it points straight up and then fill in the rest with earth.

Go into you hut. You will find on the table milk in a bowl and some honey. Tip the honey into the milk and stir it. When the honey is dissolved into the milk go to the totem and pour the milk and honey all over it and say.

> "By this offering I name <Name of the totem> as the protector, teacher and totem of this tribe."

❀ ❀ ❀

The relationship between you and the totem of your tribe is your link to the past, the present and the future. It teaches how to survive in your environment. This covers your job, family, job even your physical body. It is the tool that will teach how to rule your inner kingdom. It will not tell you about world events, or your destiny within life. That is the role of the Totem of the Nome.

When you need to speak to it again you go to the imaginary place on the Western Bank of the Nile and call it by name three times. If it comes, you ask it to 'teach you. You could ask it a direct question. Transform yourself into its form and follow it into the kingdom in which it lives. Birds fly, fish swim and desert creatures roam the desert. You will understand the answer to your question, or receive knowledge from the inner experience you have. When you have finished return to the hilltop, transform yourself back into a human and return to the village. As with all inner experiences you should write them down straight away, otherwise, like a dream, you will forget them.

Sometimes your totem cannot help you answer your question. The answer may be alien to its nature, or it is difficult to communicate to you. In such cases you will need another guide.

When this happens your Totem animal will show up, when you ask your question it will simply shake its head and go away.

You should then stand with your arms outstretched and say:

"I send my voice from the Western to the Eastern Horizon, in the land of Khem, over which Re sails his boat.
I call about the two lands and ask the Gods for the gift of an animal guide to answer my question
I ask for this that I may serve the land and the Gods."

Then you wait for another animal to guide you. Again when one appears you should ask its name. It will take you on a journey and at the end of it you should have the answer. If you do not, and it might take several journeys before you get the message, you should return to the hilltop and come back. Call for the animal guide by name and ask it to help you again. Just be aware that it might say no. If this happens you are going to have to think hard on the experience it gave you last time.

The animal guide may be with you for sometime, even for some years, but it is only with the permission of your main totem animal. Your totem animal will be with you for a lifetime, it represents what in the Western Mystery Tradition we call your Holy Guardian Angel. The animal guides are simply transitory and not as important to your life. Therefore even if you are planning to call an animal guide, which you have been working with for some years, you should always call your Totem animal first. Some of this is to do with respect, but it plugs you into the higher energies that are guiding your life. This makes sure that you never lose sight of the goal of working with animal spirits.

Sometimes you will find your Totem animal will prevent you from working with a spirit guide. This is because it might feel that you are becoming too distracted with what that guide was teaching you. If this happens you should always follow where your Totem animal leads you.

Making a Totem stick

This idea was inspired by the Maori idea of a 'godstick'. In Ancient Egypt we see various Gods carrying animal symbols on sticks that are variously identified with different Gods. It makes sense then the idea of a carved stick, or magical wand, might have been a magical tool of a shaman of an earlier period.

In his book *Tohuna Today*[3] , Samuel Timoti Robinson says the Maori used Godsticks, or whakapakoko, to call down the power of a god. If they wanted a fertile field the Maori shaman (Tohuna) would simple say a prayer and lay a godstick in field. Other times a string would be wrapped around the whakapakoko and this would be pulled to attract the god's attention as part of a ritual.

Robinson suggests that before trying to make your godstick you should first pray to the god (or as we are suggesting here communicating with the Totem animal) for at least two weeks every day. This is to form a relationship with the being. He suggests inviting the being for guidance and calling its name while you make it.

You should use wood to make the stick because it is easier to carve. Ideally the wand should end up about two feet long. Unlike the Maori godsticks, it is better to make the stick of dowel and just carve the head. Start with a rectangular block piece of wood, about six inches by two inches. Drill a hole the diameter of the of the dowel. Place PVA glue in the hole and drive the dowel into it. This should be a tight fit. When this has dried, start to carve the form of the God.

As you carve the God into the stick you should be trying to communicate with the being behind it. You could chant the name of the Totem in Egyptian.

As you carve this stick, you should remember that you are making a physical body for a God and so anything you carve is the flesh of the deity. You are "finding the god" underneath the surface of the wood and is calling it forth form its hidden house in the heavens. Shaping the figure becomes an invocation to that atua calling it into being. Robinson says that you must even treat the off-cuts and shavings of the wand as if they are holy and given them a decent burial afterwards. Although it would be good if you could get the carving looking like Egyptian gods or animals, it is not that important. It is

---

[3] If anyone is interested in knowing what real shamanic work in a Maori community was like, I can thoroughly recommend this book. Robinson knows what he is talking about from experience and his book makes the some of the ways of the Maori shaman accessible to all.

how you feel about that godform and how you create it in the wood that is important.

Robinson told me making a godstick is freeform. There are no rules about how it should look. Just shape it as you feel. You can say anything you wish to the atua as you carve and make the whakapakoko. Speak to the atua [God] kindly, as you might to a younger friend. Think positive thoughts. All of this energy enters the godstick as you cut away and let the figure take shape. Inspiration should flow when speaking of the myths as their deeds are far beyond the ability of any human."

Once completed, you should consecrate it and make it come alive still further by performing the Opening of the Mouth Rite for it.

The godstick should locked in a box and kept hidden in sacred space until needed. Do not allow another to touch it or see it.

Egyptian shamanic work, which is different from the Maori version, the godstick is used as a cross between a portable Totem pole and a magic wand.

When you have set up your sacred space you drive the stick into the ground in the centre of your sacred space. You make a private prayer to the God or animal because it houses as part of your ritual

It can be used as a magic wand when you are doing the healing or exorcism work we will be doing later.

Chapter Five

The Ancestors

The Ancient Egyptians had a world view where death and birth were not that different. Once someone died they passed into an otherworld where life was good, but part of them remained in the tomb. The bit left behind was essentially the personality; the intellect, the feelings and the various items that were not the immortal spiritual self. In Hebrew cabbalah, these 'shells of the dead' were the spiritual equivalent of rubbish. Eventually, these shells would break up, but the Egyptians and many others believed that occasionally these shells could be revitalised by a visit from the soul of the person combined with the commemoration from the family.

The Egyptian called this part of their Ancestor's the Ka and what we would consider the soul the Ba. They thought the Ka hung around the tomb, waiting for food, and families were required by tradition to visit the tombs of the ancestors on the Western bank of the Nile and provide them with food and remember their names. There are signs the Egyptians played games in the tombs of the dead.

Similar patterns of behaviour can be seen in China where there is a thriving Cult of ancestors. Most houses have shrines to dead family members and regularly leave them fruit offerings, particularly oranges. They also feel that offering food to the deceased appeases them and wards off bad luck.

The Chinese believe the dead return to visit their living relatives during the 7th month and thus they prepare a meal for them. Unfed dead became hungry ghosts and could cause problems for the township, or the family who failed to feed them. The Chinese burn fake money, paper houses and cars so the ghosts can live comfortably in the afterlife.

These events are enshrined in Chinese culture and there is a real fear by some of the older people the more modern Chinese will forget these traditions and they will starve.

During the great missionary period such practices were labelled as ancestor worship. It was assumed that in more primitive times, before humanity got the hang of Gods and Goddesses, used to worship their dead ancestors. But the real relationship between the living and the dead was more practical. At no point are the spirits of the dead ever worshipped, just their past influence is recognized among the living.

In Ancient Egypt we can see something similar in a festival called the "Beautiful Feast of the Valley" in Waset (Thebes). The festival was held in remembrance of the Dead, much like the Hungry Ghosts rites of the Chinese. First recorded during the New Kingdom, the festival shows how much of a belief in ancestors carried on for thousands of years afterwards.

Shrines of Amon were carried in a procession from Kanak on board boats to the western side of the river. There the gods in their shrines made visits to Pharaoh's mortuary temple and to the temples of other deities. Finally the statues stopped at the necropolis where rituals for the ancestors would be performed .

They gave the dead food and drink and other offerings and the deceased ancestor would be met during an all-night vigil. Flowers were given to all participants, dead as well as living with the purpose to bring the deceased nearer to the living and then there would be a party with the summoned dead.

As we roll back the clock on various cultures we see that any involvement in the affairs of the living becomes more significant, but it falls short of worship.

Once again I will provide a comparison with the Maori, who I believe, had a similar attitude to ancestors that our pre-dynastic Egyptian shamans might have had.

The Ancestors

A Maori has to know his or her whakapapa, or family tree. He must know the tribal history in much detail. This includes the migration of his ancestors from Hawaiki and the name of the tribal canoe that carried them.

Besides carrying any tribal history from generation to generation, this knowledge gives a degree of power. A person knows where they have come from and can put it in context of the land around them. When dealing with ancestors you are using an incredibly physical link connected to real people and events. You are not dealing with the souls of your ancestors, they would have long since disappeared to whatever passes for an afterlife, you are dealing with their personalities. These are identical with the shells of the dead so despised by cabbalists. The difficulty in dealing with the personalities of dead people is that they are lacking in understanding for modern issues. If you think there is a generation gap between you and your parents, imagine what it is like in dealing with your great-great-grandparents.

This might seem strange to the modern person, but we do carry our ancestors around with us in our DNA and these stretch back to the period where we were not that human. Not only are we physically like them, but we are also carrying their programming from the various psychological mistakes they made. We cannot escape our ancestors, even if we put oceans or galaxies between us.

When Maori visits the spiritual centre of their tribe, the Marae, or meeting place, there will be a statue that represents their ancestors. Some Maori will touch noses with these statues. This is called "hongi" and it is done with the living to share breath and spirit between people. A hongi with a statue of an ancestor, the act is sharing breath with the spirits of the dead. As the person does this, the deeds of the dead are remembered and invoke them into one's life.

But there is more than simple a matter of commemoration here. Ancestors are seen as being with the people of today, living with them, and having an influence over the living. A tohunga (Maori Priest) may have an ancestor who is continuing to teach him. There is a belief that his tohunga teachers, if they had not passed on all of their knowledge, can remain with them even after death to finish the instructions.

Failure to honour the ancestors was punishable by them in graphic ways. The Maori believed that a makutu (bewitching) from ancestors is common, when people fail to do so.

When a woman changed the spelling of a name on a gravestone of one of our important chiefs of her tribe and she was cursed by him and went insane. Another who started digging for some of the ancestral treasures for the hope of a quick buck lost his fingers to a mysterious wasting illness.

The Maori Ancestors claim to have an influence beyond Maoridom too. A pakeha (foreign) woman who spat on a tribal canoe, which contains the carvings of a tribe's ancestors, died young because they cursed her.

According to Samuel Robinson the woman's family asked for forgiveness, but the hara (infringement) was too serious. The Ancestors would have had a dim view of anyone who forgave such an act and would perhaps strike a makutu on the person who forgave.

But the role of the ancestors was also to protect as well. Those who have tried to launch magical attacks on Maori have found that instead of finding themselves attempting to harm one person they found themselves taking on many.

" I have also seen an instance where fifteen people were struck dead within one week by a series of 'incidents.' All of these people belonged to the same family," Robinson told me.

The relationship is not one based on fear, but of respect and love. Robinson said the ancestors are family members who are with us because they love us.

"The ancestors will curse those whom we grow angry against with reason, and the ancestors curse whose who work behind our backs even without our knowledge. The hand of makutu is strong when laid against someone because the ancestors will strike the opponents down," says Robinson.

A closer interaction with the ancestors allows some of their mana or power rub off on the modern person. However Robinson adds:

The Ancestors

> *"The ancients only have said that hospitality is the true sign of mana in a person, rather than self-gratification. The ancestors are with those who are generous, offer food to the living, take care of their families, take care of their lands, and take care of their ancestral interest."*

The Maori believed it was possible that Gods could be part of their ancestry and many whakapapa include many Gods. Also, the Ancient Egyptians believed they were created from the Gods and therefore were divine. Maori consider that because of the connection with the gods, their own blood is holy, and therefore their whakapapa shows this flow of holy blood.

The whakapapa is invoked every time the Maori introduce ourselves to another people or another tribe. In this way family lines are brought together and the mana is exchanged. They talk over ancient wrongs and fixed them. Ancient good connections run strong once again.

According to Robinson, the Ancestor's are contacted and consulted about anything that bothers a person.

Projecting what we know about other cultures, it is possible to get a glimpse of what our pre-dynastic shaman must have been doing with the Ancestors. Over time some of these traditions will have slipped away. Others traditions would be carried on throughout Egyptian history by the priests of Anu and the Sem-Priests. It is likely that during our period, a strong belief in Ancestors taking an active part in daily life would have persisted.

Contacting Ancestors

Life is short and it seems that just when we are getting the hang of it our bodies give out and we die taking all that wisdom and experience with us. Within the magical tradition we believe that none of that wisdom is lost. Some believe that when we die we merge into an absolute and, having reached the end our purpose, merge our wisdom into the collective psyche of the Universe. Others say we reincarnate with the sum total of what we have learned in previous existence, ready to learn new and exciting wisdom. Either way, we have no conscious recollection of the knowledge and wisdom of the Ancients.

Humanity's past is a bit like a dream. We have historians and clues that provide us with images of ancient times, but often we have no ideas of the context. We can see paintings of ancient rituals on the walls of temples, read ancient myths and legends but are unsure what they are trying to tell us.

The people of history are like us, but are like they came from a different culture. Contacting our Ancestors can provide the key to understanding that current of Ancient Wisdom that might link us to the past and make it more accessible to us.

There are a wealth of ideas and inventions that have been forgotten about. The world lost cement for a thousand years after the fall of the Roman Empire and an ancient Roman also worked out how to make aluminium. There was glass that would bend but not break, Damascus steel which was so hard that it could shear through chain mail and Greek fire which was a fire that could not be extinguished by water or other ordinary means. All these are skills which were lost because their time had not come yet. How many more bright ideas would your ancestors know about that never made the headlines?

There are many folk cures that are now being looked at by modern doctors; even the leach has made a comeback in to treat heart disease.

But even ignoring ancient technology the spiritual understanding of our ancestors also can give us clues about our modern lives.

How many neo-pagans would benefit from unlocking what it was like to worship in the same way as the Ancients? What was it like to take part in the Greek mysteries?

Obviously you might not be able to find out if your ancestor didn't do them, but it is possible, the further we go back in time, to find someone in your family who did something interesting.

The idea of Ancestors could be behind many 'past life' experiences that people undergo while under hypnosis. These might not be so much regressive hypnotic experiences of past lives, but channelled psychic experiences bought to us by our Ancestors

Another area that Ancestors could prove useful is as protectors.

The Ancestors

This is an area that is sliding out of modern life, which is a pity. In days were families lived in the same house for years, there was a feeling the Ancestors watched over the property. Some of this might have just been the atmosphere of history settling over an area, but as I have said before Ancestors are part of the history of your family. Now few people stay up in the houses they grew up in, let alone the places that their grandparents knew.

People who live in such places tell me that they always have the feeling that they are being watched over and protected. When this past is accepted, and the ancestors are happy, then the house is pleased.

This was bought home to me when we moved into my ex-wife's family house. We were the third generation of that family to live there and it had been built by Didi's grandfather. When we first arrived we found pictures of the family in the loft and I insisted that these be placed out where they could be seen. I also asked Didi's relatives to tell me all the stories they could about the people who had lived here.

I found out for example that Didi's grandfather thought the quality of the bricks he could buy were too poor, so he made his own from the earth the house was built on and baked them himself.

I was concerned because I was not sure what Didi's ancestors would have thought of her marrying a foreigner, or this particular foreigner had a more than academic interest in occultism and Didi's grandmother was Christian.

The house, which is on a mountainside above Sofia, had been occupied by tenants for nearly a decade. We needed to do some major renovations. Traditionally ancestors are not fond of changes and what we were planning to do involved knocking walls down and painting walls in modern colours.

To get around this problem I told the builders to use any bricks that they knocked out of the wall in other parts of the building work. In the end not a single one had to be wasted.

However I was concerned when my mother-in-law showed up and told me that she had a dream where Didi's father told her to come up to the house straight away. Concerned that in appeasing the Grandfather, I might have angered the father, I asked what was wrong. Didi's mum said in the dream he was not angry, just surprised at what could be done with the house and was pleased that we had improved the light so much. He thought she should see it.

What was strange was when we selected the paint for the bedroom I was determined that it should be a modern looking purple. We knew that Didi's mother would not like it, but was the best colour for the room and I insisted. But it turned out the colour we chose was the same that Didi's Grandfather selected when he built the house.

The house, which had always been cold and bleak, brightened and warmed up. Flowers which had been planted by Didi's Grandmother, and had not been seen for years, suddenly appeared again.

In comparison, the tenants who lived here were always complaining the electricity was constantly short-circuiting, pipes were rupturing and the rooms were always cold and damp. They were also burgled, despite have a burglar alarm; all problems that we never not noticed.

Will ancient Egypt work with my ancestors?

You might think the last thing that will happen is that your Western Ancestors will live in an Egyptian afterlife, come when called by Egyptian gods, or be controlled by Egyptian magic. However that is not true. The magic that you use, including the various godforms, is a symbolic alphabet for you. It accesses hidden powers that remain inside you and have nothing to do with the reality that is seen by the rest of the universe.

Finding the Ancestors

First it is important that you start to compile a history of your family as far back into the past as possible. This means that you should gather as much data as possible including photographs and family history. These will range from tall tales told round the Christmas table to actual newspaper articles. You should build a family tree, but more importantly, a record each 'character' on it.

This is a myth of this person's life and it should try to be as positive as possible. Everyone has skeletons in their closet that after they have died are found out. But that is less important in the shamanic tradition. If you look at oral histories, the triumphs of people are magnified and their failures all but disappear. No one cares that much that Martin Luther-King committed adultery; it was more important what he did for the Civil Rights movement. Your Uncle Sydney might have been the most boring right-wing bore in your family's memory, but his Dunkirk stories make him a legend.

There are also cases where a family member might be portrayed as a 'character' who, despite being unpleasant to live with, were quiet roguish. My Grandfather was a notorious petty criminal. It is safe to say there was not any church roof in the area where he lived that escaped the enthusiastic wretch from his crowbar when scrap lead was worth its weight in hard currency. He became a used car salesman and was so good at it, that he once was able to sell a car without an engine for more money than the same make and model with one.

Sometimes, a family member is a case study for what can go wrong – many family trees are clouded by cases of child abuse, violence and other horrors. Such stories can be carefully used as object lessons of fatal flaws or as explanations for them. Remember however much darkness they have in them, you have that same evil inside you. How you deal with it goes some way into repairing the karmic impact that your family has had on the world. However unless you are into scaring yourself rigid, I don't recommend you communicating to such types. It is enough that you admit that they are part of you and move on.

It is important to start seeing the ancestors as symbols, rather than human beings. This will give them a particular power to you. For example you can see your late grandmother as a symbol of parenthood because she managed to raise 10 kids on next to nothing and they all turned up OK. Such a figure is useful to approach when you want advice on how to deal with a stroppy teenager. Someone in the family who is a good cook would be an excellent ancestor to invoke before you bake something tricky[1]. It could be that their magic in the kitchen can flow through into you.

If you can get your family tree back far enough you will find some people to whom you are connected. For example my ex-wife has for an ancestor a Bulgar prince who ruled a large chunk of Bulgaria during the 13th century. The downside to the story is that he is regarded in Bulgaria as a traitor because he sold the country out to the Byzantines in exchange for a Byzantine princess. Either way he is a symbol of a tricky warrior which is useful. Her grandfather was a clever man who built this house from material he made himself. Recently, we had to knock down one of the walls to connect two rooms and our builders broke their tools on his brickwork so I know how good he was. He also would not let an appliance in the house unless he knew how to fix it himself. Obviously an ancestor that teaches self-reliance[2].

On my side of the family we have a string of ancestors who were usually servants to more famous people and not interesting in their own right. My Grandmother however is a strong character who was a defacto mother and matron to countless 'at risk' boys at a special school in Kent called Red Hill. As an ancestor she teaches how to handle difficult situations, never bending from doing the right thing even when it is uncomfortable. She could also swear creatively[3]

Once you have make a short story on each of your ancestors, and have made them into a fitting symbol, it is a good idea to set up some form of shrine to them. I find it interesting that people who have no interest in their ancestors, often have a bookcase dedicated to their family, often going back a couple of generations. However, if you try

---

[1] All you need to do is say "may <insert name of Ancestor> help me to do this so that I may remember his/her name upon the earth"

[2] He got into trouble with the Communist authorities after the Second World War because he stole a rusted T35 tank that he didn't think anyone needed now they had stopped shooting the Germans. He was found pulling it to bits for parts outside his house. The communists were not amused and he was jailed for a year.

[3] Red Hill School used to have trials where boys who had committed petty crimes where judged by their peers. It is somewhat telling that a boy who was charged with swearing at my Grandmother was acquitted because his defence 'she swore at me first' was accepted.

to do this consciously and with the idea of honouring your ancestors you will find the place produces a power all of its own. Therefore, I would not install such a shrine in the bedroom. Remember these are essentially shells or 'ghosts' of dead people who love the attention. If you start to get them showing up when you are trying to fall asleep it can be a little annoying.

Every month, you should try an act of meditating on the ancestors. All this takes is the simple act of lighting a candle and saying the name of each of your ancestors out loud. On special festivals, which you should try to make at the same time every year, you should make an offering to the dead and do a shamanic working of the time I describe below. We have already mentioned the "Beautiful Feast of the Valley which was held when the harvest was brought in and the flowers were ready and there was also the Feast of Wagy seventeen days after New Year's day.

To calculate when these were is a little complicated. The Egyptian New Year started when the first new moon following the star Sirius's reappearance after it disappeared under the horizon for 70 days. Sirius predicted the flood which lasted until October. When the waters withdrew it was time for planting and the harvest started at the end of February. This is a little difficult for someone who does not live in Ancient Egypt to recreate, as it is important that a Shaman work the energies of the area that surround them.

I would suggest then that you make planting time the Spring or Vernal Equinox occurs about March 21st. New Year's day the period of the Spring Equinox, Harvest, the Autumn Equinox around August 1, New Year the Winter Solstice, near Christmas. I am aware that by doing this, I am shifting the Egyptian calendar from a Lunar to a solar one, however it does make life easier.

Ancestors that are not

Before going on to look at working with ancestors directly, we should look at the idea of using ancestors that do not belong to you. By this I mean that ancestors who are not members of your extended family going down through history -- famous people that you would like to be related too. In shamanism, where you are using your ancestors, it is pointless to try to borrow someone else's family. The Chinese sage, Confucius was specific on this point. He thought it dishonourable for someone to ask another's ancestor for help in dealing with a particular problem.

The Maori would consider it downright insulting to your ancestors and as we have seen that is not something you would want to happen. This means that you should not use relatives that you are only connected to by marriage. Ancestors are all in your blood so if they have never had a chance to be there in that way there they have no connection with you. For example according to one of my aged aunts I am related by marriage to Mike Jagger. If he shuffles off this mortal coil, I would be unable to pick up any tips on vocal performance from him. Neither can I link to my wife's Bulgar prince. However if we ever have children, they could use his skills to forge a dubious alliance with Turkey.

This of course flies in the face of many modern channellers and mediums who claim to talk to dead people who give them all sorts of interesting teaching. One example of this was the famous occultist Dion Fortune who claimed that she was taught by a nineteenth-century Chancellor of England, Lord Erksine. Historically Erksine was famous for his legislation to protect domestic animals, and for having two leeches who he thought were his friends. Strangely Fortune's Ersksine failed to mention anything about animal rights or leeches in any of her channelling. It is uncertain what material Fortune might have found, had she started looking within her own ancestors for subjects.

However, sometimes people who may not have been related can be used if you had a special bond with them while you were alive. A modern example of this is the Druid teacher Ross Nichols who continued to teach one of his students Phillip Carr-Gomm long after his death.

The Ancestors

Using the Ancestors

We are now going to look at some practical techniques to approach the ancestors in a way that would be recognisable to a pre-dynastic Egyptian shaman. First you are going to need to accept some guidelines to prevent us having some nasty accidents.

First because your ancestors are dead it does not make them the font of all knowledge. Because we are dealing with shells of the dead, they can only pass on information that they knew when they were alive. If your grandfather didn't know about nuclear fission while he was alive, then he is not going to know after death. Therefore they will never know any lottery numbers, neither will they be able to refer you to ancestors who they have not met in real life.

Collectively they will have much information that works a bit like a big database and this will prove useful to you as you try to unlock the knowledge the Ancestors have locked inside you. However some of the information will be a little out-of-date. An ancestor who is a 12th century doctor would probably recommend a course of leeches for most illnesses and although he might give you a good lead on the uses of aspirin that people have not thought about.

One of the biggest problems that you will find about your database is that it does not have a search engine. You will be able to be accurate on the Ancestors who have lived for the last three generations, but sometimes it will be impossible to trace your family back more than a few hundred years if you are lucky. Then you will have to rely on your own shamanic ability and your skills to test the spirits, which we will look at later. Therefore, I do not recommend that you try approaching Ancestors who are long dead and to whom you have no material proof of existence until you have mastered the system. I also suggest that you do not talk to Ancestors from places and histories that have not been verified by scientists and archaeologists. There are several reasons for this:

> 1. Because you are opening yourself up to dead spirits, some will try to trick you to get attention. Remember some just drift around the lower astral hoping for moments like this so they

might grow stronger. It is harder for them to fool you if you know more about the person than they do.

2. Your ego will want you to find someone in the past who was someone who was important. The wish to make this happen will be inversely proportionate to the success of your own life. It would be great for a person who lives a boring uneventful modern life, to 'discover 'that they have an ancestor who was once a High Priestess of Amon-Re in Karnak if it were true. However if it isn't, then it could be a huge fantasy.

3. There is no way that you can confirm your experience. The power of the Ancestors has slight impact if it cannot be made as an objective experience. If an ancestor describes living in a village that no one has ever heard of for a culture that no one knew existed, then the rest of the information is meaningless. Of course if the message is important enough, you can visit that place, dig the site and see if you can find the village and the civilisation. But what good is it to you if you are given important information from someone who claimed to be a Priestess in Atlantis when you have no chance of proving the whole experience was a fantasy. This is not say that you snub the teaching, you just treat it sceptically.

4. Your immediate Ancestors should give you plenty of information to play with.

Most importantly your Ancestors are dead. Respect for the Ancestors is not agreeing with everything, it is just listening. They have not got the final say on anything you do. It is impossible for a dead person who lived 100 years ago to understand the sorts of decisions that you have to make now. My Great-Aunt loved children, but her husband didn't and so they never had any of their own. Despite the fact she didn't like her husband either, she stayed with him because divorce was more or less unthinkable. As an Ancestor my great-Aunt teaches me to laugh and be like a child, no matter how old you become. She would not be good at relationship advice.

Unlike the Maori, to whom Ancestors are so close you can touch them, Western Minds are better at keeping them at a distance. They do have psychic power, but not much beyond some small poltergeist activity.

Once you start to activate them, they will start to give them more power from your own personal store of energy. If you are not careful they will start to gain too much power and could cause some trouble for you. So I do not recommend you work with the same ancestor too often, not more than once a month.

Never anger your Ancestors, do not pick fights with them, argue or do anything other than politely listen. Always thank them for their advice. Unlike gods or otherworld beings, they do not have any magical ability that they did not have while they were alive. Some of them will not even know that they are dead, shells of the dead are not spiritually conscious and are a bit like robots built of from the various complexes that held them together. They are not able to read your mind, so you can politely fob them off if you have too.

The further back in history you go, the harder it will be to contact the ancestor. This is because over time the various complexes start to break down. Such a contact will appear to you, even in a spirit vision, as faded, transparent and weaker. Those with whom you have had dealings and are more recently dead will be the easiest to contact.

There are three main methods that can be used to contact ancestors. The first two we will deal with in this chapter, and the third, harder method, we will look at in the Chapter Seven

The first two methods involve working directly with the shells of the ancestor on the physical plane. The third method involves visiting the Duat or Land Of Shadows or the Blessed Abode Seket-Hetep and the Fields Of Peace Seket-Aaru and searching for the souls of your Ancestors and communicating with it.

The third method is harder because it involves finding the spirit of the ancestor in the Underworld, rather than dealing with its discarded shell. The result is much better as you are dealing with the real person rather than simply their personality. However sometimes the soul of the Ancestor will be drawn out of the Underworld, wear its old personality and speak to you. When this happens you will find that your sessions with the Ancestors are much more powerful and you have to design every ceremony as if this were your goal.

The Bulgarian Orthodox Church has a rite for the dead which is traditionally held as close to the date of death as possible. All the relatives gather in the church, a table is set up with a big picture of the dead person and much food is placed on the table. The priest says a few words and the relatives get around, eat the food and talk about the dead person. In all of these rituals there is a strong shade of the dead person standing around the photograph. Most of the time no one seems to notice them, but they just be there. Also in Bulgaria, while the cherries are in fruit, people visit the graves of their relatives and put cherries on their graves. Again the purpose of this is to remember and communicate with the dead. No one seems to know why they put fruit on the graves, everyone knows the dead don't eat, but there is no other explanation that anyone wants to think about.

If you fail to hit this level, it is not that important dealing with 'souless' shells of the dead is an important part of shamanic work.

Ancestor Contact

You should method one on each Ancestor before you try method two.

Method One

This is the safest way of approaching the Ancestors as it works through an intermediary, which is a statue or photograph. It needs two ceremonies. The first is to make the statue or photograph an effective tool using the Ritual of the Opening of the Mouth. The second is performed each time you wish to speak to that Ancestor. Once the rite of the Opening of the Mouth is completed that statue will remain as a portal for the ancestor. It should be carefully looked after. If, for some reason, you no longer want to talk to this ancestor ever again, the statue should have the name of the Ancestor removed from it before it is buried. This does not harm the ancestor, it just removes the object as an access point to this realm.

Ideally you should make yourself a statue of the ancestor and use the opening of the mouth ceremony to make it speak to you. The statue does not have to look much like the person so it does not take much in the way of skill to make. If you are unable to make one, you could try buying a small statue of a man or a woman and sticking the full name of the Ancestor, preferably in hieroglyphic (see the index) on the statue's base. If this is impossible you could use a photograph, or even a picture of the person. The ritual is improved by you holding a personal item connected to the ancestor.

After you have performed the opening of the Mouth ceremony on the statue or the photograph, you should put it on the altar you have set aside for the ancestors until it is ready to be used. When you want to talk to the Ancestor you should:

Prepare your sacred space in the usual manner. Journey in spirit vision to the shaman's hut. See yourself taking down the statue of Wepwawet and the other of Ausar. Place the statue of Wepwawet on the other side of the fire. Assume the Godform of Ausar as was explained in the previous chapter.

Relax and overlay the hunt over the physical reality in which you are sitting. Place your blanket over your head, but allow yourself eyeholes to see. Have a candle and a bowl of water in which you have placed salt and bicarbonate of soda.

Picture the statue of Wepwawet getting bigger and becoming animate on the other side of the fire.

Say to it:

"I rise out of the egg in the hidden land. May my mouth be given to me that I may speak with it before the great god, the lord of the Underworld. I am Ausar, the lord of the mouth of the tomb; and I wish to speak to the Ausar, of my Ancestor [insert the name of the Ancestor] who lives in the land of the dead."

You should see a light strike the form of Wepwawet before you. This should make it become more solid and there should be a feeling of energy coming from it. Say to him:

"Homage to thee, lord of brightness, the head of the Great House,

> *and who dwellest in night and in thick darkness. I have come to thee. I am glorious, I am pure. Grant to me my mouth that I may speak and that I may follow my heart when it passeth through the fire and darkness."*
>
> *I request that I shall speak to my Ancestor [name of ancestor] who dwelleth in the Duat. May (s)he be conducted to this place, speak to me through this image that I hold in my hands and then leave back to thy realms with my blessing."*

You should watch Wepwawet now. He might suggest that this is a bad idea, in which case, you should stop immediately. Otherwise you will see Wepwawet leave the hut. You should then say:

> *"Oh spirit of my Ancestor, the Ausar of [insert name of ancestor] by thy name I call you into the land of Khem, to live in this body I have prepared for you. Come forth in the name of the Opener of the Ways. Come forth as I call you by your old name on the earth."*

You should vibrate the name of the Ancestor until Wepwawet enters the hut again. He will have in his hands a small hawk. In your mind's eye, you stand and hold the statue above your head. The Hawk will fly from Wepwawet and land on the statue or picture. It will merge with it. Bring it down and sit with it on your lap. The statue will appear to be alive. Sprinkle it with the water and then offer fire before it.

Hold the statue or the picture in front of you. Allow your eyes to go out of focus. Now it is time to talk to the statue or picture.

When you have finished say:

> *"It is time for you to return to the Duat, I place you in the hands of Wepwawet your guide to the lands of the blessed. Thanks be to thee for thy help and wisdom, may your name last forever."*

Picture yourself handing the statue to Wepwawet who reaches inside and takes the hawk out of it. He then leaves with the hawk. Take the water and put an Ankh cross on its eyes, nose, lips and ears. Say:

> *"I seal this portal until next I wish to speak to <name of ancestor>"*

Wepwawet will return and you should thank him in your own words. Allow the light to withdraw from his image and his shape to shrink until it is the size of the small statue. Shed the godform of Ausar and place all three statues in the cupboard in the hut.

Say:

"*The ceremony is done. I come forth to the Earth again.*"

Allow the image of the hut to fade

METHOD TWO

Prepare your sacred space. Take the statue from the box. Journey to the Shaman's hut. Imagine taking the statue of the ancestor from the shelf with a statue of Wepwawet. Assume the Godform of Wepwawet and hold his godstick. Superimpose the hut over this reality.

Take the statue and draw Ankh crosses over the eyes, nose, mouth and ears. Say:

> "*I call you forth into this vessel, oh blood of my blood. Come forth <insert name of ancestor> so thy name may be remembered on the Earth and your wisdom may move among us.*"

Place the statue opposite you.

> "*Come forth <insert name of the ancestor> I am Wepwawet. I open the way for your return. By my power are you restored and by my power you shall return.*"

Hold the Godstick over the statue and see light move from inside the part of you that is Wepwawet and into the statue. Picture the statue getting bigger, but keep it smaller than you. Withdraw the wand. The image of the statue will appear to come alive. You talk to it and then when you have finished, thank the Ancestor for talking to you.

Raise the god stick above the Ancestor, see the power withdraw from it. Say:

> "*I am Wepwawet your guide to the lands of the blessed. Thanks be to thee for thy help and wisdom, may your name last forever. Now you*

shall return to the Lands of the Blessed by the power of this Totem."

The statue will shrink and become lifeless. Take the statue Take the water and put an Ankh cross on its eyes, nose, lips and ears. Say:

*"I seal this portal until next I wish to speak to <name of ancestor>"
Shed the godform of Wepwawet and place his statue and the statue of the Ancestor in the cupboard in the hut.*

Say:

"The ceremony is done. I come forth to the Earth again

Allow the image of the hut to fade.

Advanced workings

Sometimes the easiest things are the hardest and most dangerous to do. After we have worked with our ancestors in this formal way for some time, it is time to work with our ancestors so they become a part of our life without overwhelming it. Traditional shamans were able to see the spirits of the dead all around them, without fear. Their lives were remarkably similar to the film 'Sixth Sense' where the spirits of the dead could come to the Shaman to talk and be healed.

In Egypt it was believed the shells of the dead were safely tucked up in their tombs, but it was known that they could leave them and cause problems for either their families or their enemies. In fact the sceptic in me thinks the reason the Egyptians later used to bury their dead on the Western part of the Nile was because they thought that a spirit would have difficulty crossing the water. During the pre-dynastic phase the dead were buried close by and often in the houses of poorer people so the interaction with the dead was more immediate and potentially scary.

The people would have looked to their priests to act as a police force against spirits that would cause them harm. To do that, they would have to see them and only pay attention to them when they wanted.

Unlike the child in Sixth Sense, who had to put up with fearful visions of dead people in the state that they died, the Ancient shamans would have seen the spirits as unusual types of animals. In the ancestor workings we did above, the dead person was bought to you in the form of a hawk with a human head. This represented the higher aspects of the person, the Ba, which had a part-time existence in the tomb and spent much time living with the Gods. In fact the being you are most likely to be dealing with would be the person's Ka or their Khaibit which was the shadow. The Ka would look like the person and their Khaibit looks like their shadow.

You should get in the habit for looking for these spirits around you. Sometimes you catch them out of the corner of your eye and they scuttle away when you look directly at them. Sometimes when you meet people you can see the shapes of their ancestors moving dimly around them. The way to be sure of what you are seeing is to allow your vision to go out of focus for a moment and relax. You will start to see shapes around you and after a while these will form into faces. Some of these will be your ancestors, because you will be looking through your own aura. Some of these will be spirits that exist in the area that you are in (ghosts) others will be nature spirits and others will be the ancestors of others who are around you. If you manage to isolate one of these shapes, you will start to see faces in them and will be able to communicate directly with them.

This takes much practice and while you are doing it, you need a some form of magic word in your mind that switches it on and off. I suggest that you start this practice by mentally saying a word and finishing by saying another. This will help you shut down and mean that you are not cursed with seeing dead people all the time.

Ceremony of the Earthbound Dead

This is a rite that is designed to help those spirits who have become trapped on the material plane after death. Most of these are still here because they do not know where to go. Chained to the idea of mortality, they haunt material space carrying out their daily life rituals as if they were not dead. This requires a huge effort, because there are many entities that are always pressuring them to move on. The way the do this is by shrouding themselves in a cloak of materiality and ritual, making them appear like a dark cloaked figure. The effect of one of these in the room can be depressing to sensitive people. Their problem is that after you die you move onto a place that you can believe in. Such types while they were alive only believed in what they saw.

Another earthbound person stays because people on Earth will not let them go. For example one of my first experiences with such a type was when I visited the house of a friend whose husband died six months earlier. The house was thick with the dead man's presence. The wife had refused to accept her husband's death and still talked about him in the present tense. However she would be graphic about the way he died and how she intended to make the doctor pay for his incompetence. As I walked to the toilet I saw a shadow by the couple's bedroom. As I looked it took on the form of the poor husband who was chained to the bed. It only lasted for a minute, but it was clear that he was trapped here until she either won her court case or let him go.

Suicides, or people who died in extreme depression can also become earthbound. This is because depression has a similar dark cloaking effect on the aura that can be seen among the earthbound dead.

Traditionally, Earthbound dead were moved on by being remembered in churches or temples. Once drawn there by the prayers or wishes of their relatives they experience the light that stays in holy places. This light penetrates the dark shell around them and allows them to see that divine force that calls them to the next world and they move on.

Eastern churches do not hold funerals in their churches, but have rites of the dead that attract dead people to them, perhaps with the aim of helping any earthbound strays. Western Churches hold funerals in their churches and this seems also to help. Although churches claim that they do not help suicides, and there are many hauntings by suicides, it seems the divine light that builds up in churches helps such people move on.

The Ancestors

Recently because of the collapse of the church and the general agnosticism of the current age the number of points of light the earthbound dead can be drawn towards is limited. After a while, the number of earthbound dead in an area can build up. This is true of areas that have no religious place of worship such as new estates. In a few hundred years, unless some new religion starts a massive building program, the numbers of earthbound dead could be a real problem.

This rite calls all the earthbound dead within about a mile's radius into a room. Then using the godform of Wepwawet they are given a vision of Ausar. This blast of light is enough for many of them to crack open and move on. The experience can be a little scary and I have to admit I have never done this rite at night. When I wrote it another magician friend of mine wondered why English people, with little or no knowledge of Egypt would respond to an Egyptian godform. The answer is that they don't -- the Godform is for you. They would not even see the thought form that you are carefully building up. All they will sense is a feeling of light, warmth and regeneration. When the shell around them cracks, all they will see is the light and they will fly towards it.

After the rite there will be those who have not gone, perhaps because they are not ready yet. These will be banished during the closing.

A week before you perform this ceremony you should visit the shamans hut and tell the statue of Wepwawet what you plan to do. This will give the powers he represents the chance to start rounding up and preparing the earthbound dead in your area so the maximum number can benefit from the working.

The rite

Prepare your sacred space in the usual manner. Have before you incense and water containing salt and bicarbonate of soda. Visit the shaman's hut and take down the statue of Wepwawet and the statue of Ausar. You should also find a model of a small boat that is big enough to lay down the statue of Ausar within it. You should place the statue in the boat in front of you[4]

Place the statue of Ausar before you, place the statue of Wepwawet in your lap. Take the Godstick of Wepwawet in your hand. Assume the Godform of Wepwawet. You should also have the sistra handy.

Say:

> *"Behold the Jackel lord had come forth from the lands of the dead. Behold I am Wepwawet, Lord of the Hallowed Land', master of the necropolis and Khenty Amentiu, 'Foremost of the Westerners'. I have come forth to open the way for Ausar to return to my lands to be reborn."*

Pause

> *The henu boat is ready*
> *Sokaris the lord of the mysterious realm has sent his boat for Ausar.*

Picture the boat getting bigger with the form of Ausar.

Pause

> *I, Wepwawet do send my voice to the East, North, South and the West. Come forth under this place oh beings shrouded in darkness.*
> *Come forth from thy habitats of shadow.*
> *Hear the voice of the holy, the bringer to Light.*
> *Let my name bring thee*
> *Let my power draw thee to face once again the Boat of Re*
> *To withdraw to thy true place in the lands of the blessed.*

Wait a while for the dead to arrive. They will come slowly. You will also notice that they seem to be being lead by points of light. The room will slowly fill. As they arrive (and this is an unnerving experience) you should imagine the form of Ausar begin to glow white.

Take your god stick and draw the eye of Horus above the boat and say:

That which was shut fast hath been opened by the command of

---

[4] Note that there is nothing to stop you collecting these statues and models. In fact they will be extremely handy.

The Ancestors

the Eye of Horus, which hath delivered you Ausar. The light of Re is open to thee through the Eye of Horus.

Draw the eye of Horus over each of the four quarters.

> *"Shadows of the dead, the way shall be opened to him that hath power over his feet. He shall see the Great God in the Boat of Ra, when souls are counted at the bows, and when the years also are counted up.*
>
> *Let darkness not cover your faces, O ye who would imprison Ausar. Keep not captive their soul. Keep not ward over their shadow, but let a way be opened for their soul. Let them see the Great God in the shrine on the day of the counting of souls. Let them converse with Ausar, whose habitations are hidden. Let them speak to those who guard the members of Ausar, and who keep ward over the Spirit-souls. Let evil not be worked against them. A way shall be for KA with thee, and their soul shall be prepared by those who keep ward over the members of Ausar, and who hold captive the shadows of the dead. Heaven shall not keep thee fast, the earth shall not hold thee captive. Thou shalt not live with the beings who slay, but thou shalt be master of thy legs, and thou shalt advance to thy body straightway in the earth. You shall be one of those who belong to the shrine of Ausar and guard him."*

See the boat begin to glow and the statue of Ausar stand on its end

> *"Perform thy work, O Seker, perform thy work, O Seker, O thou who dwellest in thy circle, and who dwellest in my feet in Khert-Neter. I am he who sendeth forth light over the Thigh of heaven. I come forth in heaven. I sit down by the Light-god (Khu). These people are helpless, they would walk but are helpless. Let them come to thee as Ausar. Let them be drawn to the light."*

The form of Ausar will glow brighter and you will start to see the dead move into it. This will happen slowly, but you should wait until there is no one moving in the room.

Raise your wand and say:

> *"The town of Unu is opened. The head of Ausar is sealed. Thoth.*

> *Perfect is the Eye of Horus. I have delivered the Eye of Horus which shineth with splendors on the brow of Ra, the Father of the gods, You are that selfsame Ausar, the dweller in Amentet. Ausar knoweth his day, and he knoweth that he shall live through his period of life; these dead shall have being with him. As he is lifted up so shall they be lifted up."*

Raise your arms and see the boat rise into the heavens and melting into the Sun.

Take the sistrim and rattle it towards the four quarters saying at each:

> *Begone you creatures that shun the light*
> *Re has left you and you are not welcome here*
> *Begone creatures without homes for you may not live here.*
> *Think well before you approach the Light of Re again*
> *Hold no longer to thy darkness and go forth bravely*

Use the sistrum to draw Ankh crosses at each quarter. Stand in the centre and say

> *The gates of the East, West, South and North are closed.*

Sit down and shed the godform of Wepwawet.

Chapter Six

Exorcism

This next chapter deals with heavy-duty magic. Since this is not something that is played around with, and many might feel that I am wrong in giving out such techniques here[1]. However my reasons are:

- Exorcism and what is now called psychic self-defence is an important part of a traditional shaman's work and would have been important in pre-dynastic Egypt.
- If people don't know what to do when something goes wrong, they will become victims.
- One of the biggest fears that new people have in dealing with esoteric techniques is they will be attacked by entities, other magicians or become possessed. While most these people who claim they have been attacked are deluded, it does not make the situation any less real to them. As an Egyptian shaman you would have to deal with such types and you need to have the information ready to reassure them.
- To use them effectively, you will need some degree of experience in working in the inner worlds and dealing with Ancestors. Once you have this, then this work is not difficult. I have placed some degree of protection into the techniques so without the needed depth of experience, the worst that will

---

[1] One publisher rejected my manuscript for this book because they felt this chapter would get readers into trouble. My view on this is that if you are going to deal with real spiritual forces, you had better know how to get rid of the one's you don't want.

happen is the spirits in question will ignore you.

As I have given the outlines of working with Ancestors, it is possible to see how you should approach dealing with minor spirits that are a nuisance or causing problems. You might as well have the full formulas.

Sadly, there is a lack of information about how the Ancient Egyptians dealt with spirits of those who caused problems for the living. Based on what we already know of similar cultures and existing exorcism practices still being practiced in Egypt it is possible to guess.

Societies that believe in magic have a problem. They think that everything that goes wrong in life is caused by a psychic attack either by a dead person, an evil magician, or someone who has paid a magician to do it. In the Middle East, and Eastern Europe, there is a thriving underground trade for such people. Although most are charlatans, they have an important role in their cultures and provide psychosomatic cures for illnesses that have been diagnosed as psychic attacks by the alleged victims.

The use of magic to cause someone harm has been a feature of the system since before the Stone Age, but practically such attacks are psychosomatic. A person believes that a shaman has the power to kill them by pointing a bone at them and they shut down all their systems and soon die. A shaman who can convince someone they have this power can make them sick, unlucky or miserable.

One of the better 'tricks' is to say they have sent a demon, djinn or bad spirit to do the work. This means the attack is personified and soon the person will start to see a force attacking them and convince themselves they have become processed. This does not mean they are not, or the attack is minor. They will have accepted a symbol of their destruction, and by their own fear have created it. Sometimes they may have contacted a real spirit to do the magician's work for them.

In such attacks the victim has to know they are cursed, and believe in the person's power to do it. Such curses can be cured by visiting a magician who the person believes can protect them. In such cases all the 'more powerful' magician has to do is provide the person with

Exorcism

an astral sugar pill, such as a talisman, amulet, potion, or long ritual to convince the person they are no longer 'hexed' or possessed. This removes all the problems by treating the real cause of the illness, the person's belief that it is happening.

However there are other sorts of attack which are real, but are much harder to deal with by a placebo. These are cases where a person has launched an attack, or has invited the attention of spirit powers that are not exactly friendly. First let's identify the sorts of attack you could be facing.

Passive attacks

These are caused by people who are unaware they are doing it. They may dislike someone so much their emotional energy 'ill-wishes' them to an extent they unconsciously launch something similar to an all-out magical assault. For example an unemployed person and has no hope of a job may be jealous of a friend who is doing well for themselves. Left home, alone, they might project all their anger and frustration on to the successful person and wish they could suffer as much as they do. The ability of these attacks to have an effect on someone is inversely proportional to the mental state of the attacker. If they can be obsessed about anything, then they can make such an attack. The good side about such a case is that such attacks is they are easy to identify and stop. Psychically the person will appear in the person's aura and the attacks will be specific to their needs and wants. A lonely person will often attack the person through their relationship a careerless person will attack your job. Approaching the person about the attack will be meaningless, because they will be unaware they are doing it. However it is easily deflected by magical means. Most trained magicians will not have a problem with these forms of attack because the protection offered by their magical system, strengthens them against them. In this system, the guardian you have placed around the Shaman's hut will send them all packing. However other people are sometimes not that lucky.

An inexperienced magical attack

If you are dealing with someone who will sit down and bother with a magical attack, you are more than likely facing a group or individual that does not know what they are doing. Most people who have been in magic long enough know that doing magic to try to harm someone is stupid and usually comes back to bite you. There are those, and they are usually children or teens, who do play around with being a black magician and try salvaging some weakness in their egos, or they are barking mad. These people usually get hold of a book, half understand it, and try cursing the bullies at their school, or someone who didn't take them seriously. Under this heading I put 'love spells' which are designed to make the person of their dreams fall in love with them.

What most of these people do not know is that 'hexing' takes lots of energy and support. It is not a matter of doing a single ritual, making a talisman or sticking pins in images of the target. You have to do it for a long time until the person becomes sick, dies or does what you want. Unless you have close relationship with a nasty otherworld being, all the emotional power you produce swiftly scatters. Lacking the focus that years of training gives you, most of this wasted energy dissipates needs to be recharged. Low astral attacks are also killed off by the fact that as the sun rises, the world is bathed in a special spiritual energy called Akasha by the Indians. This pulls apart lower astral structures, meaning that any rituals have to be done again.

If you are being attacked by someone like this (and chances are they will be dumb enough to tell you), it is better to go to the movies or watch something funny on television. This neutralises anything the attacker can do. The next day they will have to start over. People who laugh a lot do not have problems with being attacked. Neither do people who are trained using an established magical system.

Those who are being attacked come to you complaining of a run of bad luck, or mysterious illnesses that appeared and disappeared quickly. It is unlikely that a person who has been the subject of a 'love spell' will be aware of it, but the attacker often hangs around more to see if it worked!

Exorcism

An attack by a magical group

These are potentially dangerous as instead of dealing with one person's neurosis you are dealing with a collective one and potentially a magical collective mind called an egregore. This is not as rare as it should be as there are esoteric groups who think they are important enough to carry out magical attacks on people who dare to leave their group. However in 95 percent of cases, people who leave such groups think themselves important enough to be attacked and bring all the psychosomatic symptoms of such an attack on themselves. In one public bust up I saw in one esoteric group, both sides were claiming the other was attacking them[2]. They claimed that they were only using defensive magic to stop what the other was up to.

It is the group that fears magical attacks on their group or organisation that is likely to be the one most likely to do any attacking themselves. If you are a member of such a group or organisation that has the leader constantly moaning about being attacked by other groups or organisations you should be careful.

Like the attack that is performed by the inexperienced individual, such attacks are lower astral and usually lack focus and can only give the victim bad dreams. The danger is the thought forms used by a group is often powerful enough to survive the night and continue into the next day. A person who has been attacked by a group can feel symptoms last for a long time if they are unprotected by another group, or individual. Again the spirit you have protecting your shaman's hut is more than enough to see off any attack. You will have to purify, consecrate and seal the person's aura (see the chapter on healing work) and it might be helpful for you to call for a spirit for them to see off any attacks for a while.

---

[2] One woman rang me up to complain that she had a dream where she was a dove and I was attacking her in the form of a hawk. I think she was incredibly disappointed to discover that in the midst of all the other rows following the break up of the Order , I had forgotten she existed.

Attack by a skilled magician or group

As I have said before, these are rare. The method usually involves the correct use of a malicious godform or spirit. The attacks are often not so much lower astral but use sub-demonic entities. These are difficult to control and usually take their toll on the operator. In Ancient Egypt it was possible to pay for someone to mount such an attack. Those magicians, that were not charlatans, were difficult for anyone but another experienced magician to deal with and the best way be to invoke something called the Shemshu Hor. These are a semi-mythical psychic police force, which I will show you how to call.

Attack by ghosts or bad spirits

Although this issue is not believed to be so important now, during our period it was believed that ancestors of the dead could attack the living and the shaman's would have been called into resolve the dispute. These were ancestors who felt the living were not paying them enough attention any more, were disrespectful or had failed to feed them. However they could equally be nature or animal spirits that were simply malicious. These often took the form of attacks by wild animals, snakes and scorpions. One Maori Tuhunga, I know once told me that he was once being attacked and he performed a rite of protection. Soon afterwards, he heard a scream outside his house and saw a hawk killing a crow. When it had done this, he took it as a sign the forces he had invoked had destroyed the forces that attacked him.

Protecting another from magical attack

Most people think that a magical attack is a constant battering on their aura until they are sick or dead. In fact, even an attack that is designed to make a person sick will not do this. Most attacks are in the form of energy, which psychically can be seen as images or shapes. The target of this energy is what modern magicians call the sphere of sensation, but in Ancient Egypt was the ba. The energy's

Exorcism

goal is to get the ba to accept an idea that it is not well. The ba is good at believing this stuff, as you will see in the chapter on healing. Unless it receives information to the contrary, it will go about doing suggesting the attacking person and bring about the necessary illness. But the ba does not need constant reminding from the attacker; in fact if it does it will start to rebel against the suggestions which it is being given.

So usually a magical attack will be carried out once a week until the effect happens. This is a matter of practice, I know one magician who likes to perform attacks during the new moon[3] . I assume she has found it effective, but it does mean that those people who fall foul of her know when to astrally barricade themselves in for the night.

Most are psychically attacked while they are asleep. This is because people's ba's are at their most vulnerable when the conscious mind is not around to tell them what to do. For most a psychic attack will appear like a bad dream where they get into a fight and are beaten up. This differs from a normal nightmare because the victim usually feels drained for some days afterwards.

As you can see, the skill needed for these attacks is high. This is not the case of the most common form of psychic assault, ill wishing. Unlike a direct assault this will affect the victim's life. People attacked in this way will just be incredibly unlucky.

Your first goal as a shaman should be to work out if the person is being magically attacked or not. First you should check they are not sick! Fever, low or high blood pressure, ear or nose problems can create similar symptoms to an attack. A person who has a history of mental illness can be psychically attacked, but it is more likely the symptoms they are feeling are connected to their illness:

- Dark clouds in the aura that when stared at turn into forms of animal creatures such as scorpions, crocodiles or snakes.
- The person is pale, and drawn, depressed and drowsy. They will feel like they have been drained.

---

[3] She considers herself a 'good' magician, but sometimes thinks the world is against her and a good offence is the best form of defence.

- A significant number of illnesses start to affect them and their lives.
- There have been an unusual number of minor accidents or incidents that make the person unhappy.
- The person finds themselves getting deeper into trouble financially for no good reason.
- Members of the person's family are all affected by similar events.

A Shaman needs to check, whether the person has angered someone, or has someone who resents them. If there is no one then chances are it will not be a magical attack.

You should sit the person down in front of you and go into a trance. Imagine yourself as sitting outside your shaman's hut and the person sitting there with you. In your mind's eye, look closely at the person and see what images come to your mind. You might see a person, or an animal or some symbol. You should ask the person what that means to them. You should be as clear as possible in your description to allow for no ambiguity. For example don't say "I see a bearded man" because the person may know many bearded people, living or dead. You should say "he has small glasses and wears a blue tee-shirt with writing on it". Initially, it does not matter if the person does not recognise who this person is. Next you should see what the image is doing. Obviously if the person is doing something like driving a large knife into the victim's back it is a good bet that this is your attacker. However the image could be supporting the victim, or even the attacker, but has only indirect involvement.

Sometimes you will get a group of people connected loosely somehow. For example, a friend of mine was being ill wished by her best friend.

Shamanic vision revealed there was the young woman, an older woman and in the distance there was the image of an older man. My friend, Sue could not believe the young woman would want to do her harm, however was unsurprised when the description of the older woman fitted the young woman's mother. My friend suspected the mother was beating up the other young woman with Sue's success and it was causing the emotional tension necessary for the attack.

The man however remained a mystery because he was too far back from the main action to be clear enough for me to see. Later it was revealed the young woman's father had been playing mother and daughter off against each other because he liked manipulating tension.

If you fail to see anything at this point it is unlikely the person is suffering from a physic attack. However you can still help them. This involves giving them a psychic sugar pill.

Roma fortune tellers in Sofia do this all the time, although sometimes as part of a scam. What they will do is psychically look at a person and tell them something that is accurate about them. If they look miserable or upset they will say that it is because someone has cursed them. They will then give them a herb or some junk which they say will cure them from the curse. The grateful person will give them a few dollars and walk away cured.

I would suggest a few mouldy herbs will not cut it for most people, I suggest a beads with a hieroglyphic Heru or eye of Heru, painted on it. Tell them to put it under their pillow and carry it with them for at least a month. This will give their ba all the suggestion it needs to get better. You could charge it, if you like, but you do not need to.

Once you have verified who the attacker, or the attackers, are you can work out the best way to deal with them. In cases like the one above, it is unnecessary to take on the attacker's directly. They are just being nasty and people can be like that. After a while they will calm down and everything will be forgotten.

Meanwhile you should place the person under Heru's protection. Take their full name and convert it into Hieroglyphics (see Appendix A). Write it on a piece of paper roll it up and seal it with wax or a string.

Hold it in your hand and say:

> *"I bind you oh Heru, Hawk*
> *As you were protected by Aset*
> *So shall [full name of victim] be protected*
> *As (s)he gains in strength and power*

You shall gain in strength and power
As she sees off her enemies
So shall you see off you enemies
Together, bound in protection."

Take the scroll and draw the eye of Heru[4] in the victim's aura
Vibrate Heru

The Mirror of Het-Hor

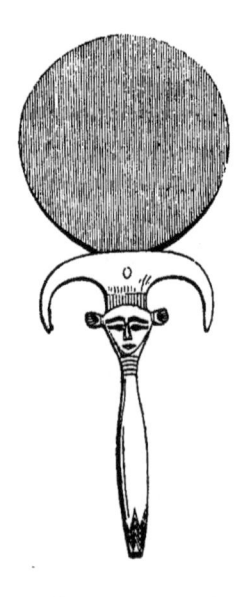

This implement is for cases where an attack needs stopping. It could be the person is employing magic, or is hiring someone to do it for them. One of the biggest mistakes that people make when they hire a magician to do their dirty work for them, is they assume that if there are any reactions they fall on the expert. This is not the case. The hireling does take a backlash if the spell fails, but most of the

---
[4] This could be done with a Heru Godstick if you have one.

magical ties fall right back on the person who hands over the money. Think of it like this, money is a symbol of power. If you hand that power over to another person who then sends it towards another with the intent of harming them, it is still your power used. If the person counters the psychic attack, the shock will pass through the magician and then onto you.

When you are hoping to shut down any attack do not focus on the rival magician or shaman, they are likely to be just as well protected as you. Instead take out the source of the power – the person who paid them and wanted the damage done first. It is safer for all concerned.

Although Aset took her role later, during pre-dynastic times, Het-Hor was the chief protector goddess. We see statues and talismans asking her to protect people from all sorts of harm including magical attacks. We have seen that her Sistium scared away bad spirits, and another one of her magical weapons was her mirror.

Egyptian mirrors were of polished metal, usually bronze. Examples found in tombs are ornate and have images of Het-Hor around the stem. The logic was that mirrors were potentially gateways into other universes and you didn't want to see anything nasty looking back at you. They used such mirrors to skry into the otherworld, which we will look at later, however but they could reflect evil energy away.

The mirror must be dedicated to Het-Hor and preferably seen use to talk to the Goddess herself.

Here is a simple ritual, which puts the victim of a psychic attack in a safe spiritual place, using the mirror of Het-Hor and a Sistium. While the victim sits in the centre of your circle, assume the godform of Het-Hor and walk three times around the circle, shaking the sistrum and holding the mirror so the reflected side shows outwards, and vibrating the name Het-Hor. You could then draw the Eye of Re in the four quarters with the mirror to provide more protection. This rite is not long lasting, but is good for preparing any sacred space if you are expecting trouble.

Using the Mirror of Het-Hor to Bind

This ritual has the potential to shut down anyone psychically who is doing any harm.

Take two copper or bronze round disks and polish them on one side until you can see your reflection in them. Draw the hieroglyph for Het-Hor on the reverse side of each disk.

Hold them in your hands and assume. Then say

Awake in Peace!
Beautiful Het-Hor wake in peace!
Het-Hor, Mistress of Iunet wake to life!
The Neters raise to worship you each day,
For you are the old one who rises as the sky!
You are the ball of the sun who pierces the sky,
Bathing the world with gold,
Who brings life in the east,
Who then immerses the setting sun each night in Iunet.
Awake in peace!

Allow the description that follows to help you build an image of Het-Hor

Your head is of lapis-lazuli, living, renewing eternally!
Your eyes, are the rays of the sun,
Your ears that hear the petitions,
To help those in this land
Your eyebrows frame the sunlight
Your lips, give the breath of life,
And spit fire against evil
Mistress of perfection, who nourishes the body to live!
Mistress of true speech,
Your throat gives the breath of life,
Filling our hearts with joy!
Your breasts of plentiful milk,
We are nourished each day!
Tambourine music and dancing bring joy to you!

Your back, stands up against your enemies
Keeping evil from those who are faithful to you!
Wake in peace!

Assume the godform of Het-Hor Say:

"I who am Het-Hor bless and empower these symbols of my protection.
May what they see be reflected.
Let all goodness be radiated from them through my symbols, but let that which harms be reflected on the person who would harm.
For as Het-Hor grows strong so shall these mirrors be strong.
Until the day that Maat has ordained, so it shall be my power that holds these mirrors together."

Write the name of the full name of the person who is doing the attacking in hieroglyphs on a small piece of paper. Place this between the two reflecting sides of the copper. Bind the two mirrors with Masking tape. Say:

"Until the day that Maat has ordained, so shall Het-Hor bind you to your own self."

Shed the godform of Het-Hor and take the disks out and bury them in the earth or cast them into a river. You much never go to that place again or try to intervene in what happens to the disks. The idea is that Maat, the Goddess of Justice, might decide to unbind that person from the mirrors of Het-Hor, because they have 'served their time'. Either way it is in the hands of the Gods and you should intervene no more.

The Shemsu Hor

The Shemsu Hor, or followers of Heru, have been described as Pre-dynastic kings, the worshippers of the Hawk who ended the reign of the worshippers of Set, space aliens and a Masonic-style lodge dedicated to fighting evil.

While they are unlikely to have been aliens, they could have been everything else. In this system they are closer to the latter. There exists in the Western Mystery Tradition the idea of an occult police force, which exist in the inner planes and sometimes work through human beings. Their job is to preserve the rule of Maat on the astral planes, and this task leads them to be the great adjusters, or balancers against dark forces.

They are called in when there are abuses of power that are too great for normal mortals to take by themselves. You do not need to do great invocations to call them; you just need a genuine cry for help.

You should be aware the first person they test will be the person who calls them. I know one wiccan high priest who was a little bit paranoid and had a tendency to overreact to criticisms from people in his coven and throw dissenters out. However he became convinced that one of his brighter students was sending bad magic against him in revenge. To his surprise the attacks got stronger and despite his magical counter strikes he was unable to stop them. Believing, mistakenly the boy had another coven to join in a magic war against him, he called on the psychic police for help. Suddenly he felt that he had lost all his power. He could not meditate, imagine or do anything. He lost interest in his group and moved away from the area. He told me that he realised that it was him who had disobeyed the Wiccan credo of "do what you wilt, but harm no one". It had been his paranoia that had led his own attacks to rebound on him threefold. "When I called on the psychic police," he told me. "They shut me down, until I realised that I was the problem." He said that it had taken him years to realise what had happened.

To call the Shemsu Hor you should draw on the ground the Eye of Re (which later became the eye of Heru). You should use a godstick of Heru if you have made one. Enclose the eye in a square. Sit cross-legged and stare at the symbol, silently calling for aid of the Shemsu Hor. When you have finished scrub out the eye with the godstick and try to forget that you have called them. If anyone asks you, do not say what you have done. The Shemsu Hor, work in silence and by calling them, you have temporary been joined to their ranks.

Exorcism

You might find that you are called to do some working for them in the future, and it may even be unconnected to the matter that you have invoked them. What they will ask, will not be serious, or even difficult[5] but you should do it as it will somehow help to bring the balance of Maat to the world. They will 'ask' in an obvious way too. It will not be a sudden hunch, or a mysterious voice in your head.

The Eye of Re can be painted onto a card, in which case the eye and the frame should be blue and the background should be orange. If you are not using the Egyptian system, and want to call the psychic police you can use a blue equal armed cross instead of the eye. I was taught that this was the modern symbol used to call them by an esoteric school I attended once, however it appears the symbol changes to suit the culture and historical period.

Possession

At times these attacks, either by magicians who used spirits, or by random attacks by the spirits themselves result in possession by them. There was a belief the dead could possess people.

This belief was so common in Egypt that it causes problems for the emerging Islamic faith. Islam believed that once a person was dead, they were not allowed to return to the living. However they must have had many Egyptians believing in possession by the dead. They believed that it was all a cunning plan by Satan to lure Moslems into taking part in un-islamic rituals, like making offerings at the tombs and having amulets to protect them from the dead.

When faced with such an entrenched belief pattern, Islam have done what the Church did and accepted possession but changed the philosophy behind it to one that was more religiously acceptable. They told people that possession was rare, and said that when it happened it was because of beings called Djinn, who were beings of fire.

However it is clear by the way they dealt with them and the

---

[5] In one case it was simply to remember the name of a famous person who had died fighting against evil. In another case a person was motivated to join Amnesty International.

descriptions they use that we are looking at a tradition of fighting such forces that goes back to pre-dynastic times.

The book, "the Sunnah" says that when a Djinn enters are person they are seized by fits and speak in incomprehensible words. If they are hit hard enough to kill a camel, they do not feel it." The Djinn controls the intellect power of the possessed in such a way the controlled loses all power to think and speak from his will. He does not remember his previous sayings or what he is about to say, he may perform certain abnormal actions, which are beyond human might.

Djinn have sensual needs and can feel love, hatred and revenge and may take over someone for the hell of it or because of some harm they accidentally done to it.

The way to remove such a spirit was through prayer and by commanding the Djinn to virtue and forbidding it from evil. The person performing the exorcism should be pure, for the force that is processing the person will use his weaknesses and sin against him.

The methods used in Islam are:

- If the possession is due to a magical act then undoing the magic will release the Spirit and stop the possession.
- Talking to the spirit and pointing out that what they are doing is wrong. Often they are not aware of what they are doing.
- Cursing the spirit until it is forced to leave
- Reciting certain Qur'aan verses or prayers
- If all this fails to work, then the exorcist physically beats up the spirit until they leave. This is done in the belief that any pain experienced by the controlled person does not feel the pain, only the spirit.

It is easy to imagine these techniques being used in Ancient Egypt with the names of earlier Gods replacing those of the Qur'ann. I should point out that if you have to get to level five of treatment it is time to give up. Historically this has caused many deaths and I doubt it works.

When we think of possession we think of the movie 'The Exorcist' or similar cases where the spirit takes total control over a person.

Exorcism

Modern minds, used to the pathologies of psychology, are a little more sceptical about these types of attack which often read like schizophrenic episodes or, even rarer, multiple personality disorder. If this is the case, the modern shaman has to be able to spot these first before crediting such cases to spiritual possession. The differences are subtle.

Here are the clues:

- A possessed person can hold a rational conversation with someone and will not skip between topics. This is common with people with mental illness.
- They will have verifiable intellectual knowledge the victim could not have.
- They will not admit they are possessed and will change the subject.
- There will be some paranormal effects around them.
- Super human strength.

Below I will give you a system to deal with them, but you must be sure that you feel confident that you know what you are doing. The moment that you start to feel that you are out of your depth, admit it and stop. If you want to see what can go wrong, you should see the film the Exorcist, or Poltergeist a few times. Most problems do not involve projectile vomit and blood pouring down walls, but such stories are based on fact, so you have to be careful.

Exorcism and the magical protection of a house or room

Rather than being the formal and heavy Exorcism rite which we will look at next, this is lighthearted. It is designed for when you first move into a house or need to remove an unpleasant atmosphere from a room, or even if you have had a long running attack of the blues. It is dedicated to the dwarf god Bes. Bes was the God of humour as well as an excellent demon destroyer. He was said to kill snakes which were aspects of Apep. This rite needs you to dance and make much noise, poke your tongue out at it and bang the Sistrim while assuming the Godform. Because it is performed in a house or other space it is a lot more free-flowing than the other rituals. It requires you to have a bag of salt mixed with bicarbonate of soda and a sistrum.

Start in a room quietly and assume the Godform of Bes. Chant his name over and over until his power starts to flow out of you. Get some active dance music (without lyrics), turn it up loud. Dance through the house rattling the sistrum making as much noise as you can in time to the music. Imagine the spirits in the house running from you. Shout Bes loudly, where you sense any spirit holding still poke your tongue out at it and fling salt at it. Work your way from the centre of the house sweeping outwards. Then chase the spirits to the boundaries of your property moving in ever widening circles. Scatter the salt on the boundary. When you have finished return to the centre of your house, raise the sistium above your head and say.

> *"This house is clean of those who would do its family harm. They may never return or they shall have Bes to answer too."*

Shed the god form and go watch a funny video or film.

Dealing with the Dead

In the previous chapter we looked at dealing with Earthbound dead. These are usually a minor inconvenience to the living and the rite shown will deal with most of them. However there are dead that have a vested interest in avoiding moving on. In almost all cultures, Ancient Egypt included, there is an idea that after death a person reviews their life and is 'judged' for their deeds. In fact this is a personal postmortem review rather than judgment by a god or goddess, but the process is always described as being potentially unpleasant. This is because a person is forced to see their lives by what they were supposed to achieve, rather than they did. Any cover-ups, blocks, or ignored reactions are critically examined. Some souls know this and will try to avoid it.

Others will feel too attached to the world. They know they are dead, but feel they must stay either because they feel comfortable, or feel they are too angry to die.

An example of this was a hotel which I stayed in Italy. It was a Gothic affair with real bats and a huge electrical storm. There was a Fellinisque feel to the place with a couple of ancient matriarchs being pushed around by dwarfs. I was with a bunch of journalists and we were a little worse for wear. One of the waiters told us that one of the floors never had guests, because it was haunted by the ghosts of some Germans who were killed there during the Second World War. Seemingly, during the war the hotel was an army hospital and was bombed by the Allies. There are challenges that drunken journalists will refuse to pass up and within a few minutes a group of us were up there with me holding a torch.

Sure enough the floor was full of the strange, mostly earthbound dead that were harmless and fortunately invisible to most of the group. As we walked around a corridor there was a door open to one of the rooms. The group, stopped suddenly. One of the groups was sensitive and said suddenly that she didn't like that room. Sure enough there was a pool of black light there. I walked towards it for a closer look. There was a feeling of anger and black fury. Suddenly there was a blast of cold air and the door slammed in my face. As I turned the torch around to say to the others "that is nasty" I noticed they had all returned to the bar for light refreshment the moment the door had slammed and I was alone. The spirit was clearly someone who was dead, knew why and resented the fact. In the end I joined my friends at the bar and made sure that night I had some of the tightest magical protection I could put on my room[6].

These types will have to feed to stay alive. They do not eat food, but survive on small amounts of energy which they drain off the living. This is the reason that in hauntings, people describe a cold wind or a sudden chill when a ghost is in the room. There is no wind, simply a decrease in your body temperature as the energy is drained from you.

This is mostly harmless, but if such a spirit hangs around too long people will start to feel tired, drained and a bit sick.

---

[6] At this point in the story, I am supposed to say that I gathered all my magical resources and sent all the spirits packing. But I was out of my depth at that time and more than a little drunk. The Universe never expects you to do more than you are capable, however much of a better ending it makes to a story.

Less harmless is the tendency to start attacking people. I have a let live and let die attitude when it comes to spirits. Most of them are harmless and evicting them from homes they don't want to leave before they are ready to do so, strikes me as a bit cruel. One house I lived in was haunted by an old man, whose only presence was the occasional smell of urine in one corner, a grumpy old woman and a cat. The grumpy middle-aged woman lurked at the foot of the stairs and I had no problem with her. For a longtime I assumed that she was just earthbound dead, but she never left the place when I did my rites for the earthbound dead. Then my girlfriend at the time had a problem falling downstairs. It was always the same stair and she injured herself badly at one point. Every time it happened she thought she saw the ghost cat first and was certain the old woman was around. She thought the old woman didn't like her, and said I should perform some exorcism, which I did using a technique which I now don't think effective[7]. The old woman, the cat and the urine smell disappeared for about six months and then the cat came back. I moved out soon afterward so I am not sure if the other's returned eventually either. Whatever the old woman was, she didn't like my girlfriend and was determined to get her out of the house.

An Egyptian shaman's job would be to make sure the dead either went back to their tomb, or carried on their journey into the afterlife. The exorcisms and banishings so beloved of modern magicians then were only used in a last resort.

When you are dealing in cases of haunting you need first to make sure that you are safe before you start approaching any dead spirits. This you can do by purifying and consecrating a small circle in which you sit. If it is consecrated you can lay your blanket on the ground and further strengthen this by opening sacred space on it.

You should leave enough unconsecrated space for the spirit to appear in the room. Any consecration ceremony raises the spiritual pressure of the room. Beings that are lower astral cannot take much in

---

[7] It pushes the beings out of the house with a burst of energy. It removes the problem for a time, because the lower astral spirits are pushed out, but does not provide a cure.

the way of spiritual pressure and will not enter such space. Normally this is good, but in this case you want to talk to someone and they have to be close for you to hear them. Do not make your sacred space so large that you will not be able to speak to them

While the exorcism work carries on, you should not step off the blanket or leave your sacred space - even if the spirit in question starts lobbing household objects at you.

In addition you should have a mirror and a sistrim of Het-Hor and a godstick of Anu.

The room should be flooded with candlelight and incense. This will enable the spirit to become more solid.

While performing the rite there are five possible outcomes:

1. Nothing happens.
2. The spirit comes and doesn't say a word.
3. The spirit comes talks and is cooperative.
4. The spirit comes talks and is uncooperative and or leaves.
5. Spirit attacks.

It is more common that nothing happens. If I could make dead spirits appear on demand I would be showing them to people who have offered large bounties for people who can do that. Spirits may not show up because they do not exist, they do not have the power to do so, they know what you are up to and are hiding in the woodshed, or simply do not want to talk. There are ways of compelling spirits into a circle, but since I do not think that is a good idea and more likely to result in you getting attacked I am not going to say.

When spirits do show up they sometimes don't talk because they lack the skill to do so. Talking is what we do on the physical plane. When you are on the lower astral it becomes replaced with telepathy. Some spirits don't know that and try speaking as they would when they are on earth. You have to show them. Other times they do not speak because they don't want too. You have to try to convince them. Those that talk and are uncooperative have to be warned that life will get unpleasant for them if they do not start being a bit friendlier. However avoid making threats. They work about as well as any earth threat and will have to be backed up.

It is important that you get the spirit's name. Most western spirits will tell you it without thinking. This is because most of us have forgotten how important our names are. Once you have the spirit's name, often you can stop them stomping off, or make them return. Usually saying the name is enough, writing it down on a piece of paper will create a talisman that works a bit like a classic voodoo doll.

Next you should find out why they have been unable to move on. This could be simply they have been trying to get a message to a loved one, or do not like something that is going on in the house. This is common. I was once asked to clear a house of a spirit of an old man who had lived there before. He was furious the house had been taken over my students, who had ignored his garden and destroyed the atmosphere of calm he had striven to keep when he was alive. He had no family and died alone. He was attached to was his garden. In the end the students agreed to tidy it up and the ghost seemed happy and moved on.

If the spirit is angry you should just listen. Remember some of them have not had the opportunity to state their case for years. You should then ask them what could be done to make them happier and help them to move on. If they don't know, give them a few suggestions. If it needs you, or the people that live in the house, do what is suggested and then call the spirit again. If it does return ask it why, after you had done all that was needed, the spirit was still there.

The Ceremony

Equipment

You will need those two mirror's of Het-Hor that we described earlier. Do not use your regular mirror. You will need the Sistrum of Het-Hor and the Godstick of Anu. The room should have many candles and be flooded with incense to help you see the spirit. Other than this, it should not be lit. Lower astral beings have a problem with electric light, which helps scatter them.

Exorcism

Make your sacred space and then visit the hut, imagine the hut being placed over the physical space. In your mind's eye take down the statue of Het-Hor and Anu.

Assume the godform of Anu:

> *"I who am the Opener of the Ways*
> *Stand at the gates of the world*
> *And call forth the spirits of this place.*
> *Come forth ye without a voice*
> *Come forth and speak to the God of the Dead"*

<Pause to see if anything comes. If nothing does then take the godstick and twirl it chanting the name Anu for a minute.>
Repeat verse and wait. If nothing happens then repeat the twirling of the godstick and the chanting of the name Anu. Then repeat the calling. If nothing happens this time say the following.

> *"I who am the Opener of the Ways Will leave this place.*
> *No longer will your voice be heard before the Gods.*
> *Instead you will be left on earth as a shadow of what you were*
> *Slowly fading, your name will be forgotten.*
> *Come forth, Come forth I say."*

(If nothing happens now you should wait a while before closing your circle. The ghost, if it is there does not want to talk. If it does show up then it is a matter of talking to it and finding out its name and what it wants. If it becomes uncooperative, and you know its name, you can say:

> *"Spirit of <name> I who am Anu say listen to my words (and or return) and answer my questions."*

If the spirit needs help in moving on you should say the following

> *<Name of spirit> rises out of the Egg in the Hidden Land. His/ her mouth is given to him/her that he/she may speak with it in the presence of the Great God, the Lord of the Tuat. Let not his/her hand or arm be repulsed in the presence of the Chiefs of any god. <Name of spirit> has become Ausar, the Lord of Re-stau. May he/*

she whose word is true, become linked with Ausar who is at the top of the star ladder. According to the want of his/her heart he/she goes forth from the Island of Nesersert, and has quenched the fire of life.

I who am Anu, the walker between the worlds, shed the skin of the sem priest and lead this Ausar into the Tuat. I openeth his/her path on the eastern horizon of heaven and he/she shall alight towards the western horizon of heaven, I shall carry him/her and he/she will be. There is food in the heavenly mansions of heaven which his/her divine father Tem hath established. It pleaseth me to grant to <name of spirit> the power to float down and to sail up the stream in the Field of Reeds (Sekhet-Aaru) and reach Sekhet-hetepet (the Field of Offerings)].

Shed the godform and see it leading the dead spirit away from the shaman's hut and into a boat on the Nile. See Anu push the boat and then sail it into the sunset.

Spirits that do not go quietly

If spirits start to cause a problem, refuse to go, refuse to say why, start attacking people then you are going to have to say the following.

"Spirit. I have come to help you. But I warn you that your behaviour is out of place among the land of the living. Therefore I must ask Het-Hor to take you from this place by force. Do you choose to fight us?"

If the spirit does not calm down then it is time to get heavy. To do this you should use the Godform of Het-Hor. But because the case is a little more dangerous you should use a more powerful identification with the Goddess than you have done so far. Each line should be said while rattling the sistium. This weakens the spirit. While you are assuming the Godform of Het- Hor. Say:

*"I awake
I am Het-Hor the Beautiful
Mistress of Iunet
I awake to life!*

Exorcism

The Neters raise to worship me each day,
I am the old one who rises as the sky!
I am the ball of the sun who pierces the sky,
Bathing the world with gold,
I bring life in the east,
And Death at the setting sun
My head is of lapis-lazuli, living, renewing eternally!
My eyes, are the rays of the sun,
My ears that hear the petitions,
To help those in this land
My eyebrows frame the sunlight
My lips, give the breath of life,
And spit fire against evil
I am the Mistress of perfection, who nourishes the body to live!
I am the Mistress of true speech,
My throat gives the breath of life,
Filling our hearts with joy!
My breasts of plentiful milk,
We are nourished each day!
My back stands up against my enemies
Keeping evil from those who are faithful to you!

If the spirit has fled you should command it to return. You will find it is compelled.

Hold up one of the mirrors of Het-Hor so it reflects the spirit's image. Say:

"Spirit[8] By this sacred and holy mirror, I have captured thy image.
Your shadow now belongs to me. It has been trapped in my mirror."

See part of the ghost flying into the mirror.

Het-Hor hath eaten your shadow.
As your shadow hath been captured, so shall thy Ba be captured.

Picture another part of the ghost flying into the mirror.

---

[8] If you know the name of the spirit you should use it, wherever I use the word spirit.

As your Ba is captured so shall your Ka be captured.

Imagine another part of the ghost flying into the mirror. All that should be left is a spark of white light, you might see this in the form of a heron.

Your soul is free spirit
Your soul is free to fly
Begone from this place oh soul, rise into the heavens with Re.
For I shall take thy ba, ka and shadow to where it may do no harm.

See the spirit fly towards the heavens. Take the other half of the mirror and place it on top of the other. Seal it down. Take the sealed disk as faraway from the house as is possible. Ideally it should be west of the house with a river between you. Dig a hole as deep as you can make it. Place the disk in the centre of the hole and put a flat rock on it. Bury it saying.

"The place which is closed is opened, the place which is shut (or sealed) is sealed. That which lieth down in the closed place is opened by the Ba-soul which is in it. By Het-Hor the Spirit is delivered.

Ornaments are established on the brow of Re. His/her stride is made long. He/She walks over a long road. His/her limbs flourish.

He/she is Heru, the Avenger of his Father. The road of souls is opened. His/her twin soul seeth the Great God in the Boat of Re, on the day of souls. Het-Hor hath delivered for him/her soul.

Light is on the faces of those who joined to Ausar. His/her soul shall not remain captive. The way is open to the Spirit's soul and shadow. The Spirit seeth the Great God in the shrine on the day of counting souls. It repeateth the words of Ausar. Those whose seats are invisible, who fetter the members of Ausar, who fetter Heart-souls and Spirit-souls, who set a seal on the dead, and who would do evil to this spirit, shall do no evil to him or her.

Haste on the way to the spirit. Your heart is with you and your heart-soul and Spirit-soul are ready and they guide you.

May you sit down at the head of the great ones who are chiefs

EXORCISM

of their *homes. The wardens of the members of Ausar shall not hold thee captive, though they keep ward over souls, and set a seal on the shadow which is dead. Heaven shall not shut thee in."*

Chapter Seven

Underworld Landscapes

In *Magical Pathworking* I explained how the mind creates an inner world for itself which acts as a magic mirror for our unconscious. By journeying into this reality and interacting with the creatures we find there, we can understand ourselves and improve. I added that as you got deeper into this reality it shifted from being personal and subjective, to something more universal and objective.

Shamanism has always trodden in these worlds, although it is only in the 20th century that psychology has given us the words to describe the process they were going through. Not only did the Shaman describe this inner landscape as the underworld, they said it was the place where the dead journey when they die.

The Ancient Egyptians drew various maps of this underworld at various times of their history. These include the Pyramid Texts, the Coffin Texts, The Book of the Dead, The Amduat, The Spell of 12 caves. There was also the book of Gates, The book of the Netherworld, The book of Caverns, The Book of Earth, The book of Night, The book of Day, and The Book of the Book of the Heavenly Cow. They have a lot in common and any changes reflect the different religious ideas of the time.

The first maps of the Underworld were drawn on the Pyramids of the Pharaohs. These Pyramid, Coffin and Book of the Dead texts are a little less coherent than some of the later works written in the New Kingdom. This is because they are describing formulas and spells which are to be said at a certain point in the journey of the Soul. The New Kingdom works of the Book of Gates and the Book of the

Amduat are a lot clearer for our purposes, although I have included aspects of the early books where possible. Using these as guidelines, it is possible to build a uniquely Egyptian underworld that has the advantage of being a subjective and objective reality. Some of the material from these books has been adapted by my own experiences and so may differ from the Egyptian material and your own experiences. You should see the notes below as a Hitchhiker's Guide to the Duat, rather than a detailed, or scholarly analysis. There will be those who complain that I have taken names of Gods, details and other information from too many different sources. They will argue that it is not an accurate map of the Ancient Egyptian underworld. However as any Egyptian scholar will tell you, there is no such thing. The Egyptian underworld changed throughout history. There was no time when it was purer or 'right'. I have based the various passwords and place-names on what I have experienced there myself – they might be wrong, but they worked for me. This fits into my belief these Underworld experiences start as being subjective and become deeply personal visions of a 'true' reality. Other Egyptian shamans getting something different from me only proves rather than weakens this point.

While visiting these kingdoms the Shaman will discover much about him or herself, the world, and the mystical forces that work behind the scenes. They will meet the souls of their ancestors and totems in a much deeper way than they are able to do with other visualisations.

Each division will reveal four different pieces of information.

- The personal world and experience of the Shaman.
- Information about death and rebirth.
- Spiritual initiation and enlightenment.
- Magical techniques and occult teachings.

Before you go

Before you pack your astral luggage there are a few important things you should know. The symbolism that you are dealing with are, for ow, bigger than you. It is important to be polite with such beings. Although they want to help you, the part of you they seek to help is not the personality, which often makes smart comments, can be disrespectful, or arrogant[1]. These beings are Gods and cosmic forces, they do not have to help you and sometimes they will not.

The AmDuat and the Book of Gates both divide the underworld into 12 different sections or kingdoms. These kingdoms were all visited by Re (the Sun) in his boat as he passes by them each night. Re spends an hour in each one and at various points' drops off passengers and brings his light to the dead. Each division has a door or a gate. A guardian protects each gate and will insist on a password before letting you pass.

The journey is dangerous as there are servants of chaos who will try to stop the boat. In one of the final hours there will be a huge battle with the Egyptian chaos demon Apep which if Re loses will result in the Sun never coming up again. So frightened were the Ancient Egyptians of this, the temples conducted rituals all-night to help the Sun God win. Sometimes the fight would be so difficult the morning's sky was blood red.

You will find that many of the symbols described in these journeys will seem strange to you. That does not mean they will not start to work a deep magic on your psyche. The more you travel these paths, the more information on what these symbols mean will become known to you. I have put footnotes after each Pathworking to help make some of it clearer, but like interpreting a dream, most of it will be up to you.

Obviously it would be too involved for you to experience every hour of the underworld each time you want to visit it. I have written a pathworking where you board the boat of Re and then allow yourself to sleep until you approach the part of the underworld you want to visit. Once you have visited it, you can fall asleep and wake up with the sunrise.

You will notice that I am giving you the barest outlines of these Kingdoms. The difference between Shamanic work, and other

---

[1] Of course that could just be me.

Underworld Landscapes

esoteric systems is that it stresses the individual views of the shaman. If you see Old King Cole in the fifth hour, it is up to you to work out what to do with him or her and what he or she represents to you.

You should always start and finish your journey at the Shaman's hut and in consecrated space. For all workings of this type you should make a Godstick of Re.

During each Pathworking you will meet the guardian. The guardian will send you back if you do not know his or her name. You should memorise this before you go. In my experience, the guardian appear when you have run out of intellectual ideas about that part of your inner kingdom and real intuition is starting to teach you. You will know if you have not met a guardian that you have not experienced what that particular kingdom can teach you.

Those of you who are familiar with the AmDuat and the Book of Gates will notice that there are some significant changes. In some cases this is a merging of the ideas of the two texts, in other cases it favours one over the other, and in other situations it is completely different. This is based on my own explorations and what worked for me.

The Beginning

Taking the Godstick of Re, walk out of the Shaman's hut and to the Nile. Standby the bank and soon a large boat will row down the River. You will see there is a bright light on board. It comes from a shrine in the boat's centre. It is the crown of Re.

This is the Sektet boat. It will stop at the dock and let you on board. On the prow of the boat is a red feather which radiates power and calm. At the head of the boat is a Ram headed God called Af. Behind him stand Anu, a human looking god called Sia (Divine Knowledge) and Het-Hor.

Behind the shrine stand five gods, Heru, Shu, the human Nehes who acts as a lookout. By the rudder is the golden god of Magic, Hu. He greets you and asks you wish kingdom of the Duat you wish to journey too. He will point out a spot in the boat in which you can sleep. The boat sails on:

THE FIRST DIVISION
NET-RE

Guardian: Arnebaui
Guide: Ushem-Hat-Kheftiu-Nu-Re

Gods flank the boat. There is the god Neken who holds a spear in his left-hand, Ausar, Sekmet and a Ram headed God called Sehetch-ur. You are arriving at a small port. Before you is a beautiful field called Maati. Re gives each god and goddess a place in the field.

Re leaves the boat and walks through the fields and you follow. Soon you will come to a City called Net-Re. Re will shape shift so he becomes Ram headed. As you follow him you realise that he is followed by a line of nearly dead people. He enters a temple courtyard. The dead remain here but you can follow. Re enters a huge temple with a throne where the altar should be. Here there are nine Ape gods who open the gates to the Great Soul. There names are Un-Ta, Ba-Ta, Maa-En-Re, Abta, Ababen, Aken-Ab, Benth, Afa, and Tchehtcheh.

There are 12 goddesses who open the doors in the earth. There names are: Qat-A, Nebt-Meket, Sekhit, Ament-Urt, Sheftu, Ren-Thethen, Hekent-Em-Sa-S, Qat-Em-Khu-S, Sekhet-Em-Khefiu-S, Huit, Hunt, and Nebt-Ankh.

There are 12 women, who guide Re. Their names are Tentenit, Sbai, Mat-Neferu-Neb-Set, Khesefet-Smatet, Khuai, Maket-Ari-S, Urt-Amt-Tuat, and Her-Ab-Uaa-Set, Mesperit, Ushem-Hat-Kheftiu-S, Sheset-Kerh-Maket-Neb-S, and Teset-Tesheru,

There are Nine seated gods. Three are human; Hetch-A, Maa-A, And Hes-A. Three are jackals; Neb-Ta-Tesher, Ap-Uat, and Ap-Sekhemti and three are crocodiles; Tchat-Tuat, Seki, and Sekhem-Hra. They fill the room with Praises for Re.

Underworld Landscapes

There are 12 snakes who throw fire from their mouths and make light in the darkness of the Underworld. Their names are Besit, Hetepit, Ka-Mut. Khut-Mu, Heseq-Khefti-Set, Nefert-Kha, Mert-Neser, Behent, Ap-She, Nesert, Ap-Ast, And Shenit.

Re says to them:

"Open the doors and let me come into your Courts! Give your light to me, and make yourselves guides to me. You have all come into being from me and my word has expressed through you. You are made of my body and I have fashioned you from my soul."

And the Gods reply:

"Re, the doors to the secret Amenti are open before you. The doors of Nut are open wide. Shine in the darkness. The people of the Duat shout for joy as you enter the Gates of the Earth."

The dead are judged before a totem of a jackal and a totem of a Ram.

Re orders the Gates of Net-Re be shut behind him and you board the boat with him.

Comments

This is the first Gate on entering the Underworld. It is the state between waking and sleeping, the material world is close this one and has a great influence here. What you are looking at hear is the process of changing your consciousness. The guide is the Goddess Ushem-Hat-Kheftiu-Nu-Re who is connected to Het-Hor. What this hour teaches are the bodily processes of falling asleep and how to exist on the edges of the real and the unreal. You learn how to make your magical worlds co-exist with the real worlds. Because this is the place of Sunset, it is the place where you learn to accept the passing of things that are not relevant.

You will find the newly dead here, usually the night following their death. It is here the first judgment of their life begins. The name of the field is Maati after the goddess of justice and balance. Each of the Gods and Goddesses are assigned her powers.

The gods and goddesses named here are powerful guides to opening various aspects to you in this state. The Apes are the nine aspects of spiritual wisdom and the 12 women who 'open the gates of the earth' are the 12 signs of the Zodiac as they work on the material world. The 12 goddesses who guide Re are the higher aspects of spiritual astrology. The group of nine made up of seated humans, jackals and crocodiles are the three aspects of humanity; the crocodile (reptilian), the jackal, (animal) and the human (higher consciousness). The fact they are praising Re shows these aspects must be tuned towards the Spirit. The 12 snakes that light up the Duat are the 12 aspects of spiritual energy. Re purifies and strengthens all these different aspects.

This realm teaches how to protect yourself magically and physically if you are in danger. It is a safe place if you feel attacked. Neken, Ausar, Sekmet and Sehetch-ur are particular good as guides. The Am-Duart says that whoever has knowledge of this part of the Duart shall have magical protectors for him or her on earth. These protectors shall also act as magical protectors for him or her in the Great Duat.

Finally this place teaches you how to penetrate the subconscious underworld that you are creating.

THE SECOND DIVISION
URNES

Guardian: Am-Nebaui
Guide: Seshet-Maket-Neb

As you wake up you will notice that besides the normal gods there are two huge snakes on the front of the boat. These are the Goddesses Aset and Nebt-Het. When these two are together the bring about the power of resurrection and healing of some kind. The fact they are in their serpent form suggests the healing is physical.

In front of your boat there are four others. The first boat represents heaven and has a full moon resting on it. There is the Goddess Maat on this boat.

Underworld Landscapes

The second boat, between two goddesses is a huge sistrum, which is the symbol of the goddess Het-Hor. The Third boat has Anu in it. He guards Ausar in the form of a large lizard. In the fourth boat there kneels an armless woman and standing behind her is a man without arms. The boat is packed with corn. In the centre is the God Neper, who is a form of Ausar as the God of Vegetation.

The boats stop at a jetty. There are a multitude of Gods and Goddesses here and they are all armed. They have two jobs. The first is they act as messengers between this world and the Gods and they work to overcome those fears of the dark. The do this by reflecting the light of Re when he has left. They draw their power from the Sun at Night as he passes them by.

Also here are the Gods of the seasons who supply sacred plants for the gods and offer water to those who follow Re. They kindle fire with which to burn Re's enemies.

The gods of the Tuat are overjoyed that Re has returned to send forth light in the darkness which is in the Underworld.

Re replies that everyone in Urnes should open their doors so the darkness may be thrown aside and they can receive water of healing and food.

Comments

Here is where the shaman will learn the arts of healing with herbs and water. There are many gods and goddesses here who will teach him or her. The methods of Egyptian healing involve lunar, planetary and divine actions which can only be activated by the solar healing energy of the sun. Sometimes this involves leaving potions exposed to the sun. Other times they made potions during certain phases of the moon.

However another important part this part of the underworld is understanding techniques for protection and defense. In Net-Re this protection was passive and involved shutting and locking doors, in Urnes this is much more practical and offensive. My impression here was this was the hour where those that fight evil come to rest and gain strength before going out and fighting again. It is a place you can come to gain your strength and heal up when you feel that life is getting you down. The warrior gods and goddesses can warn you of coming problems that you might face.

The book of the Duat says that if you know all the secrets of this part of the underworld you will be protected from harm in this world and the afterlife.

THE THIRD DIVISION
Net~neb~ua~kheper~aut

Guardian: Khetra
Guide: Thentent-Baiu

When you wake up you find the boat has pulled up alongside a battlefield. These are the fields of the Peru gods who you met recuperating in the last division. You will notice the boat of Re has taken on a more martial appearance and is protected by the Hawk, Heru.

There is another boat which has three aspects of the Hawk totem, Heru, Bak and the Goddess Baket. They are protecting a third boat which contains Ausar who is lying down in the form of a mummy. The last boat carries a form of Ausar, this time with the head of a Ram. The battle is over, indeed it will only start again long after the Sun has left the Duart.

The Boat of Re lands.

There are many Gods here, they are called the Baiu-Shetaiu and they are loud and seemingly aggressive until they know you. You know the name of the Guardian of this part of the Duat which will prevent you from coming into any harm. They have the role of fighting evil. It is through the sacrifice that is symbolised as a battle here that Nut come into being and the Nile flow.

There is another section of this part of the Duat where it is not good. Here the Baiu-Shetaiu have the job of separating the soul of the dead from their ba and ka. There are many fiery pits here which

Underworld Landscapes

make it look like a prototype for hell. In these pits the shadows are cast. Everyone that does not know the name of the Guardian is thrown into one of these pits as part of purification, until any evil within them is burned out. Again the name of the guardian Khetra will protect you.

In this part of the Duat, away from the battlefield and across a stream there is a great city to Ausar. Here people are allotted lands if they fight of the cause of Good.

The city of Ausar is much more pleasant as a place where the souls rest after they have been through their purification.

Comments

This place is the original heaven and hell together, with the emphasis being on the hell. The place is dark because it represents a part of the afterlife experience where the soul judges itself according to the standards it set before it came into incarnation. In the astral worlds emotions and passions, good and bad, are energy. In this place the Gods help the person to strip away that those parts of themselves that are not immortal. This is similar to being burned and would be painful, if you hadn't left your nerve endings in your body. However it is cathartic in a dead person because it means that all their weaknesses and failings are stripped off them and burned up.

The reason that this area is a battlefield is because the tendency towards evil and chaos shows more in some souls than others. If it were not for the mercy of the gods in beating it back, souls which have drifted too far towards this tendency fall into evil. Any good they have done, and everyone has some good in them, would be lost to the shadow sides of the universe for some time.

Here is the place the Shaman goes to understand more about the darker sides of their personality. It is under the guidance of the Baiu-Shetaiu and Thentent-Baiu they can shed those aspects of themselves that are no longer important and are standing in the way of a fulfilling life.

THE FOURTH DIVISION
Tchetbi

Guardian: Sokar
Guide: Urt-Em-Sekhemu-Set

This part of the journey is different because there is a measure of threat here. The danger does not come from the snakes or serpents of Apep, but rather the ancient God of the Dead Sokar. Even Re travels this place carefully; in fact in the book of Gates he takes a detour around the Kingdom of Sokar. It is the place of dark shadows, whispering dead and above a sense of time that settles on the place like a thick fog. The only way to pass through this land is to avoid fear and always remain balanced. It is scary.

When you wake up you will see the boat of Re is being towed by gods and goddesses that you cannot see. The boat will turn away from the Nile and into a short canal surrounded by dark sand covered mountains. You will see fiery snakes moving across the hills. Finally you will come to a massive door, which is big enough to take Re's boat. However you will have to get out of the boat, which can now see is being dragged by the gods Tun-En-Maa, Her-Uarfu, Ar-Nefertu, And Shetai.

The door is called Mates-Sma-Ta and when you vibrate the name it swings open to reveal a canal called Re-Stau. Re-Stau is the pathway of hidden things, it is called the Holy Way. It goes through the Sokar's body. Thus you pass through him and never see him. In fact all you see is mist and fog and the whispering voices of people on either sides of the path. You can only see because Re's boat lets out flames. You will see shadows move closer and then run away again. Re-Stau is sacred to Anu who is leading you through some of the darker experiences you will have here.

However you will meet some important teachers, can giving you much knowledge. They are:

- Neith; a serpent, with a human head, and two pairs of human feet and legs; three serpents, which move side by side along the

ground "on their bellies".
- A scorpion called Ankhet; a three-headed serpent, with a pair of hawk's wings, and two pairs of human legs.
- Anu, who holds a scepter, in his right hand.
- The serpent Neheb-Kau, which has two heads at either end of its body.
- A headless god called Ab-Tuat; Nekhebet
- Two women called Muthenith, And Shatheth,
- A divine mummy called Bennii;
- A lion-headed goddess called Hen-Kherth
- A goddess, with a pair of horns on her head called Thest-Apt
- The Serpents Amon and, Hekent
- A three-headed serpent Menmenut.

There is no guide named for this part of the Duat so you will have to find your own.

Comments

It is a puzzle why the God Sokar gets such a bad press in the book of Gates and the Book of the Amduat. Other than these two documents, there was nothing to suggest Ancient Egyptians feared him. He was just another God of the Dead. His name means 'he who lives in his sand hills'. For a long time I thought that it was a fear of death, being expressed here. But the descriptions lead to a serious of symbols that can be scary. If you have ever been alone in the sandhills after dark, you will understand that any sound carries and you end up speaking in whispers.

My experience of getting off the boat and exploring was of a direct experience of any fears that might bubble to the surface of the unconscious. Finally, in the centre, deep in a dusty pyramid lies Sokar in the form of a mummy, alive but dead.

As far dying goes, this is the place of eternal sleep, of shadows in a graveyard, similar to the Greek Hades. It is a trap for the soul who expects nothing of the afterlife other than an ending. It is where all knowledge stops and calm settles. Many people can live much of their afterlife with Sokar, who will finally awaken them from their dreamless sleep and send them onwards.

It is not surprising the priests of Re built a way through this Kingdom, using the force of Sokar himself to help the soul strengthen itself rather than become trapped in Sokar's land. This hour of the night is a place to find Wisdom, either from the shadows you find or from the Gods and Sokar himself. This area is dangerous, because we meet our fears, and for some these are overwhelming. But it is the place where we find our power.

After the trials we may experience in this hour of the night, we will see a vision. This is something similar to the initiatory experience of seeing the Sun at Midnight

In the centre you will have a chance to see a vision of the coming morning sky. This is an initiatory experience and not much can be said about it until you have experienced it, and then you will be a little short on words.

THE FIFTH DIVISION
Tchetbi

Guardian: Teka –Hra
Guide: SEM-HER-AB-UAA-S

The Fifth Division is guarded by nine gods, who are described as the "Fourth company". They stand at a gate which is called Arit. There is a jackel, called Aau at the entrance to the corridor and another at the exit called Tekmi.

Flames come from the boat of Re to purify the corridor. The Nine gods say that Re-heru-khuti

Teka-Hra guards the gateway here in the form of a large snake that stands on its tail.

Re will say: "Open thy gate to Re-KHUTI, that he may bring Light into the darkness."

The Gate will shut after the God has passed through it. You will notice the boat is being towed by twelve gods called the Baiu Reth-Ammu-Tuat, or the "the souls of the men who are in the Tuat".

Underworld Landscapes

The party will be attacked by the snake Ennutchi here but everyone will be protected by the Baiu Reth-Ammu-Tuat who will succeed in binding it.

Re and the boat is greeted by many ancestors. These are the righteous who have lived according to the rule of Maat. They live off Re.

There are many temples here and the light of the sun feeds them as the boat passes. Here are the 12 Kheru-Ahau-Em-Amenti, Gods who make stable the path of life and have the word of the palace of destruction. It is these who decide when someone will live or die in the Underworld

There are the Eight sovereign Chiefs in the Duat who write the life of souls who live in the Duat. They are so powerful that offerings are made to them by the living while they are still on the Earth.

Comments

This is one of the heavens that exist for the Ancient Egyptians. Entrance however is blocked by a smaller version of the serpent of Chaos. It seems that just before the dead enter this heaven, they face a moment of confusion where they are destroyed. The danger is that many will be, because they might believe they deserve it.

You will notice the boat of Re purifies the corridor before he enters. This is to remove as much evil as possible from those who might be standing in the Chamber. Again only the 'good' get passed this level and others who are not ready yet are turned aside.

The underworld legal service is starting to crank up in this division in readiness for the Judgment Hall of Ausar in the next one. The 12 Kheru-Ahau-Em-Amenti and the eight Chiefs of the Duat have the power of life-and-death in the Underworld. They essentially find the dead shadows a place and will work out when they will start to fade. As far as the dead are concerned they still have much of their personality intact. The Kheru-Ahau-Em-Amenti are assigned to a sign of the zodiac and are therefore in charge of the date of the trial. It is possible the se are vestiges of an astrological calculation of when the dead person had made the Judgment Hall. The Chiefs have the job of telling shades when it is time to give up the ghost. It is from here the various religions of the world are 'fed' with spiritual energy.

A Shaman will find the spirits of the Dead and Ancestors here who have lead a reasonable life. It is a useful place to understand religions and the powers they can bring. Here all religions have their temples and are lit up by the sun. If you think about this as a symbol, it means that all religions exist within the unconscious mind, but all have as their motivating force a single spiritual light.

THE SIXTH DIVISION
The Judgment Hall of Ausar

Guardian: Set-em-maa-f
Guide: Mesperit-Ar-Maat

The god's boat comes to a pylon gate which stretches across the river and passes through it. The boat is pulled along a corridor until it is stopped by 12 gods and goddesses. These ask Re to open the hidden place.

He raises his arms and a door at the end of a huge corridor is opened to reveal a massive room.

At this point Re dies on his throne and is carried to the throne and placed on it. He becomes Ausar holding an Ankh cross in his left hand and on his right he carried a sceptre.

His throne is on top of ten steps. On each of the first nine there stands a different God. On the tenth step there is a huge pair of scales.

As the room is entered there is a loud squeal and a pig runs towards you. It is chased away by a dog-headed Ape with a stick.

All who enter the Judgment Hall must measure their heart to see that it is not unbalanced by too much evil. If it is there is a man behind the scales with a large axe to deal with the person.

The soul is judged and if they are found wanting, they are hacked to bits and their 'body' fed to the serpent of Chaos.

Comments

It may seem strange that judgment takes place after the paradise of the last division. However as far as the dead are concerned, the previous division was all about having a well-deserved rest after all the adventure of dying. The dead have already done a little self-evaluation, but this is limited by the fact they are still closely attached to their lower aspects. They can only measure their performance in life by their own standards. This can be a little confusing, but take for example the people who worked in Hitler's death camps. Their personalities, built by hard brainwashing, would consider there work to have been for the greater good. It is technically possible these monsters, if they were not dealt with by earth plane justice[2], could get this far into the afterlife still believing they deserve some reward.

The Judgment Hall of Ausar measures the person by a cosmic standard. This is a huge difference, and although the system is benign in many ways it is ruthlessly fair, which is a little different from being a walk over.

In the Judgment Hall, Ausar judges through the agency of the Goddess Maat, who is represented here by her scales. She is cosmic justice and order personified. Although it is Ausar who rules the Hall, it is Maat who is the real judge of the soul.

The dead person's heart is weighed, not against a feather of Truth, as in the Book of the Dead, but against their own evil acts (represented by a bird). In otherwords you do not have to be perfect, your good has to outweigh the harm you did to the Universe.

Before you enter the Hall you must purify your self by saying the following. It must be true, because any untruth will weigh on your heart later.

I have not done crimes,
I have not mistreated animals,

---

[2] Earth plane justice does give the personality a reminder that it has, somehow, done something wrong. The symbolism of a law court forces the person to wonder if they have done something a bit wrong. Of course this doesn't work if they are acquitted.

I have not conscious tried to do evil.
I have not sought forbidden knowledge
I have not done any harm.
I did not begin a day by exacting more than my due,
I have not offended the earth plane authorities
I have not blasphemed another's god,
I have not robbed the poor.
I have not done what God hates,
I have not maligned an employee to his or her boss.
I have not caused pain,
I have not caused tears.
I have not killed,
I have not ordered someone else to kill,
I have not made anyone suffer.
I have not interfered with the way another person worships
I have not taken anything that belongs to the gods,
I have not stolen from the Ancestors
I have not used sexually unwisely
I have not shortchanged another person
I have not taken another's land for me
I have not been dishonest in business
I have not tried to interfere with the rule of law
I have not lied in court
I have not taken milk from the mouth of children,
I have not deprived cattle of their pasture.
I have not ignored the holiness of sacred places
I have not interfered with things that are holy
I have not prevented another from receiving a blessing
I have not stopped another from getting their basic needs.
I have not quenched a needed fire.
I have not neglected the ceremonies of the gods.
I have not denied the gods their due
I have not stood in the way of the will of the Gods.
I am pure, I am pure, I am pure, I am pure!

When you enter your lower self, which is represented by the evil pig creature tries to stop you from being judged. It knows that any control it may have had is now over. It is driven away by Tehuti. This is a symbolic representation of the soul's own wisdom. It knows it has to be judged and it is ready to do so.

The form of the proceedings is not given other than in the Book of the Dead. This is the Negative confession, or rather declaring innocence. In the real world we can rationalise our sins, but in the Hall of Ausar the meanings of these confessions are taken in their widest possible sense. I have modernised them so they make more sense to modern people.

Then there are the 42 questions and these are put by Gods of Justice called the 42 Assessors. It is clear from the descriptions the se are connected to the early Totem animals of various towns in Early Egypt. This was then probably a swearing by the Totem animals of all Egypt that goes back to our period. There is a description of each Assessor above the Question which I have again modernised. They will approach you silently and you must then tell them that you have not done the sin they represent. If you cannot say the line, you should not pretend you can. You should be as honest as possible.

The wide walking God who comes from On:
I have not done evil.

The Flame-grasping God from Kheraha God:
I have not robbed.

The Long-nosed one who comes from Khmun:
I have not coveted.

The Shadow-eater who comes from his cave:
I have not stolen.

The savage faced oen who comes from Rostau:
I have not killed people

The Lion-Twins who come from heaven:
I have not shortchanged anyone.

The Flint-eyed One who comes from Khem:
I have not cheated.

The Fiery-one who comes backward:
I have not stolen a god´s property.

The Bone-smasher who comes from Hnes:
I have not told lies.

The One who throws flames who comes from Memphis:
I have not stolen food.

The Cave dweller who comes from the west:
I have not sulked.

The White-toothed who comes from Lakeland:
I have not destroyed God's property

The Entrail-eater who comes from slaughterplace:
I have not extorted.

The Lord of Maat who comes from Maaty:
I have not stolen food from another.

The Wanderer who comes from Bubastis:
I have not spied.

The Pale-one who comes from On:
I have not talked too much

The Villain who comes from Andjty:
I have fought only to protect myself and my family

The Fiend who comes from slaughterhouse:
I have not committed adultery.

The Examiner who comes from Amsu´s temple:
I have respected my body.

The Chief of the nobles who comes from Imu:
I have not caused fear.

The Wrecker who comes from Huy:
I have not trespassed.

The Disturber who comes from the sanctuary:
I have not been violent.

The Child who comes from the nome of On:
I have not been deaf to the law and balance

The Foreteller who comes from Wensi:
I have not quarreled.

Bastet who comes from the shrine:
I have not turned a blind eye to evil

The Backward-faced One who comes from the pit:
I have not harmed a child sexually

The Flame-footed One who comes from the dusk:
I have not been false.

The Dark-one who comes from the dusk:
I have not reviled.

The Peace-bringer who comes from Sais:
I have not been aggressive.

The Many-faced One who comes from Djefet:
I have not had a hasty heart.

The Accuser who comes from Utjen:
I have not attacked and reviled any one's god.

The Horned-one who comes from Siut:
I have been careful in the way I have used words

Nefertem who comes from Memphis:
I have not sinned, I have not done wrong.

The Timeless-one who comes from Djedu:
I have not stirred up trouble.

The Willful-one who comes from Tjebu:
I have not polluted the water

The Flowing-one who comes from Nun:
I have not raised my voice in anger

The Commander of people who comes from his shrine:
I have not cursed a god.

The Benefactor who comes from Huy:
I have not been boastful.

Nehebkau who comes from the city:
I have not been haughty.

The One who is High-of-head and who comes from the cave:
I have not wanted more than I had.

The Captor who comes from the graveyard:
I have not cursed my own totem

In the mid 1990's Dolores Ashcroft-Nowicki penned a ritual which was based on the Judgment Hall. In it she emphased the presence of the Goddess Maat and creatures called the 42 Assessors who she saw as expressions of the questions. It was a grand ritual with a cast of hundreds. I mention it here because the ritual was famous for having a deep life changing effects on the candidate. Usually they needed to go off and do some significant work on their personality or marry someone else. These are the experiences you have when you start measuring yourself against cosmic justice and the readjustment that you should expect.

I would suggest you put yourself through this division as one who is dead at least once a year. By confession what you have done, you are able to put it all past you and move on. By holding the evil in your heart you make it heavy when it is measured on the scales.

This division may be used to ask the Gods and Goddesses for justice or help in dealing with the law, if your case is just. Just remember it is no good hoping the Gods will help you if your case is anything but just. You will pass the Maat current through yourself long before it displays on the earth. This means that you will be judged and bought into balance if you are found wanting, just by evoking help from here.

In *Magical Pathworking* I gave an example of how the Judgment Hall could be used to help heal victims of abuse who had no recourse to proper legal justice.

THE SEVENTH DIVISION
Bekhkhi

Guardian: Akha-En-Maat
Guide: Khesef-Hai-Heseq-Neha-Hra

The dead Re starts to awaken. He is escorted by Jackal headed stakes with the bodies of the Re's enemies bound to them. The entrance of the seventh division is guarded by beings called the Seventh Company. Also guarding the gate is bearded God called Shepi. The gateway is called Pestit which once opened reveals a corridor. This corridor is purified with flame from Re's boat.

Once entering Bekhkhi you will see on the left side the enemies of Re being purified by fire on the left hand bank. On the right you will see the Just people made perfect. They will wear an ostrich feather in their hair to mark they have past through judgment. They are empowered by the light of Re.

You can see on the right hand bank, the God Ausar giving the people corn.

Comments

This phase is a consolidation of the last. Re is now alive again, but only just. His followers celebrate their victory, and enemies are punished. This might seem a little barbaric to modern eyes, the torture of 'evil' souls which is a little too reminiscent of medieval Christianity. However, nothing ever dies. Once a soul has been purified it is sent back to the Halls of Judgment. This is a repeat of the process the dead went through earlier and it is much harder because the standards of cosmic justice are a little higher.

The Egyptian shaman will find the souls of much older ancestors here. Because we are dealing with souls, rather than shells of the dead, we find their knowledge is much broader than the younger ancestors. This is because, after being so close to the God they have learned a little more about how the universe works.

It should be remembered that this is not the final paradise of the dead. Although there are many who will be content to stay with the God Ausar, which is a euphemism for being reborn. Ausar is a corn king, who eternally renews himself. Re, on the other hand, is reborn into the sky which is a more spiritual path. The rest of these divisions are for those who wish to travel this spiritual path with Re and become something 'more than human' that is a God-human fusion.

THE EIGHTH DIVISION
Aat~Shefsheft

Guardian: Ab-Ta
Guide: Nebt-Usha

Re gives those dead who have remained with him clothes of white. It is in this division the dead start to be resurrected with the healing powers of the sun, which is growing ever stronger. He calls to them by name and they are awakened.

Here the dead are resurrected with new bodies being built either for an earthly incarnation or a spiritual destiny.

There are nine beings here. They are have a large knife, and from the curved end of each is suspended a human head. They are the nine servants who help in the resurrection. Their work is find those things that prevent a natural of resurrection and protect the newly reborn dead.

Their names are:

- Hetep-Ta.
- Amon.
- Sesheta-Baiu.
- Sekhen-Khaibit.
- Neb-Er-Tcher.
- Mennu.
- Mathenu.
- Metrui.
- Peremu

Comments

This place is especially useful to magic that involves bring dead objects to life, such as talismans. In such an instance you can journey with the talisman and have it awakened by Re, when he reaches this division. You could ask the Servants to protect the newly formed talisman and make sure that it could do its work.

It is a good place to see if there are any past life links between your ancestors and people around you now. The servants remember who has been brought to life as what.

Finally it is a good place to gain power to fight serious life threatening illnesses as it is the place where the life force is born in the dead. Your guide will help locate the best time and place to do this.

THE NINTH DIVISION

Tcheserit

Guardian: Sethu
Guide: Nebt-Usha

There is a city called Bes-Aru here and the Sun-boat is carried by the Gods who live there. Now the dead are fully reawakened and able to move. They have Heru bodies, which means they are able to travel between this world and the next.

They use words to bring life and strength to Re and utter words on his behalf in the chamber each day.

Here there are 12 serpents whose task it is to provide magical energy to the body that will help it be reborn either in the world or in the next life. They have the job of destroying those things that are not in Re's plan. Their names are:

1 Amon-Tuat (Aries)
2. Tekait (Taurus)
3 Shu Tefnu (Gemini)
4. Khut-Tuat (Cancer)
5. Tertneshen (Leo)
6. Ap-Shet (Virgo).
7. Ankhet (Libra)
8. Shen-Ten-Amm (Scorpio)
9 Meri-Em-Satet (Sagittarius)
10. Aat-Aru (Capricorn)
11. Nebt-Uauau (Aquarius).
12. Nebt-Rekeh (Pisces)

There are Nine bearded gods, who holds the symbol of "life" in his right hand, and a staff, the upper portion of which is in the form of a snake, in the left hand. These Gods are under the control of Heru-Her-She-Tuati "Heru who is over the lakes in the Tuat."

1. Sekhti (at the base of the spine)
2. Am-Sekhet-F (groin)
3. Nehebeti (two inches below the navel)
4. Tchamuti (Navel)
5. Neb-Aatti (Solar Plexus)
6. Heq-Neteru-F (heart)
7. Pan-Ari (Throat)
8. Teser-Ari (Between the eyes)
9. Aha-Sekhet (The crown)

Comments

There are two key things that are happening in this division. The first is rebuilding the dead and giving them new bodies. Neither the Book of the Duat, or the Book of Gates, describe this and the zodiacal and charka attributions are purely my own work. It makes sense when you consider the template for either a spiritual being or a new physical is being built here.

It is my belief the energies of the zodiac and each person is imprinted with a special energy pattern that represents this new life. When they are reincarnated they will be born at a time that reveals this astrological pattern. If there rebirth is initiatory or spiritual the energies will affect the spiritual work. If these Gods are worked with slowly and carefully, they can help you correctly display their energies in your current life. They can be a good cure for physical illness and other energy workings, which we will look at in the next chapter.

The 12 serpents could be used to impress a zodiacal power on a talisman that was designed to attract something within their power. They could be used for healing.

Here the dead are given their spiritual wings. You incarnate with these and these enable you to travel between worlds when you astrally project or are asleep. Those on a spiritual path learn to use them to arise between heaven, the underworld and the material world. The Egyptian Shaman would learn how to use the spiritual wings they were born with to climb these realms.

The Tenth Division

Shetat-Besu

Guardian: Am-Netu-F
Guide: Tentenit-Hesq-Khakabu

There is a city here called Metch-Qa-Utebu, however this is where the battle against Aphophis, the supreme Egyptian evil takes place, you will often feel a bit distracted.

The entrance to this division is guarded by sixteen uraei. Like before, you will come to a gate that is guarded by a bearded, mummied form called NEMI, who holds a knife. He guards a corridor which is consecrated by flames of fire, which go from Re's boat.

This time the boat is piloted by Heka and Sa and there is a procession of Gods in front of it. These include Unti, a human time god, Hawk, Sereq (another human god), Abesh (human) and Lion.

Then there are three star-gods who each old a star in their right hand and, the winged snake Semi. Anteater stands on the bows of Re's boat.

When Apep attacks he will be caught in a net by the Gods Aset, Neith and Serket, and Monkey helped capture the monster with magical nets. He is restrained by deities including the earth god Geb and the Shemshu Hor.

Sometimes the battle will be lost and Re's boat will be swallowed. When this happens Set will cut a hole in the stomach of the serpent and free him.

Comments

Apep embodies Chaos. He is not likely to have appeared in pre-dynastic times as there were no representations of him until the middle kingdom. However the system needs to have a bad guy, and Apep is a good way of having a balance to Maat, who is embodies Order and Harmony.

At a superstitious level it could be that Ancient Egyptians thought that if Re didn't complete his journey the Sun would not come up and everything would be dark. Some think the times that Apep succeeded in swallowing the Sun accounted for solar eclipses. This idea is not practical it meant that Apep had to be following Re into the daytime. All Apep's battles were fought in the Duat, at night, when no one would see them.

It is more important to see that Apep's victories are always short-lived. It is a symbolic no matter how chaotic things get, the light and order will always win.

Apep is a powerful force for the Shaman to carefully understand. It is the ability within everyone to destroy what has been created. Sometimes this is necessary, to build new forms, but construction does not interest Apep. The way the gods control him is with magic, order and discipline. Here you will discover your urges to destroy everything you build.

As far as the those seeking to unite with the true spiritual sun are concerned, Apep is the force of fear that blocks them on their spiritual path. It is the limits in their humanity that always fights them.

As far as those seeking to reincarnate are concerned, it is the sudden lack of nerve that accompanies the new soul in wanting to achieve its spiritual targets for incarnation. But Apep can only slow the march forward, he is unable to stop it. Thus with discipline and self-belief he is bound.

The Eleventh Division
Tesert-Baiu

Guardian: Sebi and Reri
Guide: Sebit-Neb-Uaa-Khesef-Sebiu-Em-Pert-F

There is a city here called Re-En-Qerert-Apt-Khat. Here the bound body of Apep is dragged to the Temple of Het-Hor by Geb and the Shemshu Hor. The Goddess appears in the form of a Cat and cuts it to pieces. The pieces are then gathered and tied up with a strong rope. A huge hand comes from the Nile and pulls the rope, until the pieces of Apep are dragged under the water.

Re is with the Star Gods who will escort him on his rise into the heavens. But before he moves on he turns his boat to face up the river and sheds his light throughout all the Underworld.

He transforms himself into Beetle (Kheper) and prepares to rise into the sky. He is then crowned as King of the New Day.

Comment

The forces that prevent the rebirth of the sun and, by symbolic association, the initiation of those on the spiritual path and the rebirth of the dead, are finally removed. Het-Hor in her role as an exorcist destroys the snake and binds him. It is from the temple of Het-Hor in Re-En-Qerert-Apt-Khat the techniques of exorcism are taught. Visiting there can teach you much about dealing with evil and chaos. The rope that binds Apep is time. Whenever we are faced with periods of chaos, we can limit its impact by adopting a good Saturnian discipline.

Here the followers of Re prepare to climb with him and become more than human. It is from these Ancestors that we can learn much. However finding an Ancestor who has been raised to this level might be hard work.

It is the time that those beings who are preparing to reincarnate are communicating with the body which is being made in the womb of a living being. If a shaman is called on by a pregnant woman who wants to know more about the soul of her child, this is where you will find it waiting.

The Twelfth Division
Tesert-Baiu

Guardian: Pai
Guide: Hu

Re in the form of Khephra approaches the gates of the Eastern Horizon. There stands a bearded mummied being called Pai. He opens the gate into a corridor which leads to the dawn. The corridor is swept by flames of fire from the boat.

This leads to the Kheper-Kekui-Kha-Mesti, the city of the Golden Dawn. There the boat is changed to the Matet Boat which arises between the thighs of the Sky Goddess Nut and into her realm. He is with the Gods Seb, Shu, Hek, Hu, And Sa, who are transformed into birds.

Comment

This final gate is more of a launchpad into the sky. It is an initiation and a transformation for anyone who goes through it. I do not recommend you enter this gate without going through all the others first. Initiation is something that happens deeply to those who are ready to experience it. Shadow initiations are like shallow romantic relationships. They seem like a good idea at the time, but eventually are soon forgotten as the real thing appears. Therefore, you should thoroughly explore the Underworld and your own self before you try it. What happens beyond that point is so transcendental, it is difficult for anyone to write but a glimmer of what they have seen.

Here is the moment of physical birth for the reincarnating soul. It is possible to help the child go through this difficult passage by seeing him or her off at the gates of Kheper-Kekui-Kha-Mesti. If you do not chose to rise with Re, this is the city where the shaman learns about beginnings and births. It is the place where the light of Re, empowers the new body and personality they will have built for themselves in the underworld. It is the place where they will always find their personal power, even in the depths of depression.

Chapter Eight

Healing and Magic

Egyptian magic was legendary for its elaborate ritual drama, so much so the Ancient Greeks considered the rites themselves 'mysteries' and considered themselves to be 'initiates' if they were invited to attend. These elaborate displays, where the Priests and Priestesses enacted the myths of the Gods, were a far cry from the much simpler magical workings being practiced on the streets. Yet, it is clear from the fragments of spells that we have had written down for us, the magicians who were still making charms and talismans for people, were closer to our Egyptian shaman.

Both borrowed each others techniques. Some of these, such as assuming god forms, may not have been performed with the same robes, masks, or music, but are still recognisable.

In this chapter I will outline a simple approach to magic which might have been familiar to our Egyptian shaman, some I have harvested from actual magical papyrus and others are modern inventions.

There has always been a fundamental belief that humanity has the ability, through different techniques, to change the environment around them without using physical means. Each culture has developed a belief in Magic, even during its most scientific periods. Few have managed to say what it is, although bright sparks like Alistair Crowley and Dion Fortune have made a good stab at it. My definition is that magic is the art and science of becoming a co-creator with God. It is a wide idea, but as far as our shaman is concerned he or she would be hoping to use spiritual powers to create

Healing and Magic

new circumstances for him or herself, or the society around them.

In Egypt this was done by 'sympathetic' magic. The term was first coined by the great anthropologist and comparative religion expert Sir James Frazer (1854–1941) in his book *The Golden Bough*. He said there were two kinds of sympathetic magic – something that mimics the wanted object, and something that is based on contact with the object.

According to Frazer the principle, of Imitative or Homeopathic magic is that "like produces like" and an effect resembles its cause.

In other words if you have made an image of a person and injure or heal the image you will harm or heal the person.

In the Ancient Egyptian legend of the Evil Shepherd Hai, a slave stole a magical book belonging to the Pharaoh Rameses the Great. Using it he made wax images of people and love charms. When he harmed the image he would say "It is not wax that I am destroying. It is the liver, heart, and spleen of my victim."

However the use of such images was mostly used for healing. So if a person was suffering from a headache in a particular part of the skull a doll would be made with a pin placed in it where the pain was. Then, the shaman would adopt the godform of Aset or Het-Hor, and say:

"As this spike is withdrawn, so shall the evil that hurts <the name of the patent> be withdrawn"

The pin would then be ceremonially destroyed to make sure the pain did not return.

Stones of various colours that resemble the illness could be placed on the body. Jaundice would be sucked up into a yellow stone, scarlet fever into a red one etc.

Another homeopathic technique, which is a little dangerous in my view, is for the shaman to mimic the symptoms of the illness in their own body. Then imagining the illness as a demon, or an animal they expel it from their body magically and mimic perfect health. This is a little dangerous as it is possible the Shaman might identify with the person's illness and will become sick.

The natives of Central Australia would mimic their totem animal, while holding a symbol of it. The idea was to encourage the totem to appear to them, usually so it could be eaten.

Fraser defined the other branch of sympathetic magic as 'Contagious Magic' it works on the idea that once an object has touched another it remains linked for a long time.

So if you have in your hand a lock of someone's hair, you have control of the person.

Taking these two principles together it is easy to understand the workings behind Ancient Egyptian magic. Take for example the importance attached to the idea of knowing a being's name. If you know a person's full name and write it down, you have created a full symbolic representation of the person and can perform sympathetic magic with it.

If you know the name of a God, it gives you the ability to control that being and force it to do what you want. Chant a God's name often enough and it must pay you attention. It is not surprising that magic has always had a bad press with organised religion who are more for devotion to their god or goddess rather than ordering them about . But they are missing the point, something that can only be understood when you have done much work with different godforms. It is possible to see the Gods in two different ways. One is the symbolic expression of a myth or force that is to be worshipped and the other is a personal relationship with a fragment of the universe which is much bigger than the rest of us. If our Ancient Egyptian shamans didn't believe in the Gods and Goddesses being universal powers because they could order them to heal a festering scab then they would not have called them to heal. The relationship between the two beliefs is symbiotic. Magic cannot work if you invoke something you do not believe or have some relationship with. The magician depends on that relationship to take control of what the God or Goddess does[1]. They believe in the energy the God or Goddess has and are focusing it using techniques that appear

---

[1] There are lots of references in the Pyramid texts of Pharaoh threatening to eat the gods if they do not do what

Healing and Magic

like commands. More often they are not commands either. For the Magician assuming the god form of a God or Goddess is working with them. Any commands are then the result of a symbiotic union between the God and the shaman. This is why my definition of magic is 'becoming a co-creator with God'; you are working with the commanding power of a fragment of infinity to create something new.

Timing

There is a long tradition of magic being carried out during certain hours of the day. This recognizes energies flow better at different times.

The Ancient Egyptians believes that certain gods controlled certain times of the day. From a practical magic point of view, the Shaman would be aware of this and take advantage of it. The hours are calculated by finding the time of sunrise and the time of sunset and dividing the time by twelve. This is because the hours will get longer and shorter according to the seasons and what would be the hour of Isis in summer might be the time of Heka in Autumn.

Hour	God or Goddess
1	Maat
2	Hu
3	Sia
4	Asbet
5	Igaret
6	Seth
7	Horus
8	Khonsu
9	Isis
10	Heka
11	Ankh-neteru
12	Anu

If you are performing a ceremony or Pathworking during daylight, you could use the power that is available at the time the ritual starts. If you were doing a rite for protection you could use the hours of Horus or Anu and ask them for help in making it happen.

The Goddesses of the hours of the Night can also help, we looked at these in the last chapter.

Healing

One of the most important principles with magical healing is that it not only has to be done, it has to be seen to be done. It is not the shaman, or any gods or spirits they may call to help them that do the healing. It is the work of the patent. Any powers the shaman calls to aid the patent simply give them something practical to work with, once they allow the healing process to take place.

Many of the illnesses that people face exist first in their mind. This is not the same as saying illnesses are all in the mind. It is saying that our mental habits lead us to experience physical illnesses. These mental habits built up over time and are difficult to shake. Curing a person is not simply a matter of treating the symptoms; it is a matter of dealing with the mental causes behind such problems. I deal with some effective methods to tackle with such issues in my book 'Magical Pathworking'.

A shaman can help a person find out what these causes are by journeying to the Duart and talking to the right gods or beings found there. However this is a risky business as it does not allow the patent to take part in their cure. This limits the effect of any healing work.

Also under no circumstances should you try to suggest that this approach is a substitute for modern medicine. It should be seen as complementary as it will work alongside any chemical treatment.

Diagnosis with Het~Hor Mirror

I have developed a spirit journey below which will work to help the patent find the cause of the problem. This is more emotionally risky for the patent but will lead to a more dramatic effect.

First you have to offer to take them on a spirit quest and lay them down in your sacred space. You should have a few candles lit and incense.

Next, you should tell them that you are going to take them on a spirit journey and they should follow you in their mind's eye. They should pay attention to everything they see so they can tell you afterwards. If you know their spirit animal, you should include it into the Pathworking as a guide.

The spirit journey

You are lying on a bed on a large reed boat. Above you the sky is blue and you can see a hawk spiraling. Sitting up, you can see that you are floating on the River Nile during ancient times.

The boat is docking at a holy place which is surrounded by a wooden stockade. You leave the boat and walk into stockade. You find that it is a small circular building, about the size of a modern house. This is what an early Egyptian temple looked like before there were pharaohs in the Ancient land. Before the temple is a totem pole with the head of a cow with large horns. You walk past the pole and enter the temple.

It is dark in comparison to the light outside. There is an overwhelming smell of incense and you can hear the gentle bells of a sistium being rattled.

As your eyes adjust to the darkness and you can see a priestess, wearing a cow skin cloak sitting on the floor cross-legged. She is flanked on either side by priestesses carrying sistriums.

This is the priestess of Het-Hor, the cow goddess of healing and protection. She asks what you seek and you tell her what it is that you need healing.

She nods and claps her hand to a curious beat. The beat is then taken up by the priestesses with the sistium and soon the room is filled with a jangling rhythm. Follow the rhythm and breath with it. Relax

<pause>

After a while the priest tells you that your illness has a cause deep inside your unconscious. The Goddess Het-Hor knows this and invites you to look into her mirror. This mirror will take you back in time before the spirit of the illness became physical, and to when it first appeared in your mind as a rogue idea.

She holds out a mirror which is made of polished copper. Even in the semi-darkness of the room you can see your own face in it. She chants the name Het-Hor and soon the reflection in the mirror starts to change. You are looking into a scene from your past. This was when you first felt the idea that became the illness. Remember this scene.

<pause>

The mirror clouds again and the priestess turns it once around. You can see your face again. Now she says when you look into the mirror again you will see a symbol. This represents the spirit of the illness. It does not matter what you see you must remember it.

<pause>

The mirror clouds again and the priestess turns it once around. You can see your face again. Now the priestess says the Goddess Het-Hor will give you a symbol that represents your cure. Now she says when you look into the mirror again you will see a symbol. Again it does not matter how strange it is you must remember it.

<pause>

Now the Priestess tells you that you must return to your own time and place so you can bring about your cure. You thank her, stand, and walk out of the temple, and to the dock where your boat is waiting. As you step onto it, the boat mysteriously sails itself into the middle stream of the Nile. You lay down on the bed again, the sun is starting to set. You shut your eyes, and when you open them again you will be in this time and this reality and you will remember all you have seen.

Working it Out

The shaman must try to interpret what the patent sees as if it were a dream. The first scene could give an accurate assessment of when the illness began, but it is more likely to be clouded by the person's intellectual assessment of what might have caused it. However you must take this into account when you work out your diagnosis. The symbol they get for the spirit of their illness is more likely to be accurate, but it will want some thought. For example if they say the spirit of their illness was Raven you might wonder how their illness could be seen as a big black bird. So you ask them to come up with some associations with the Raven they might have. Word like black, bird of death might appear. So, perhaps we are looking at an illness born out of a fear of death. Sometimes people are so frightened of dying they react toa snuffle as if it were the Black Death. Such types, rather than reducing their own illnesses get much sicker.

The symbol of the cure needs some lateral thinking and a requirement for the person to tell you want it means to them.

Direct healing techniques

If the cure suggested by Het-Hor fails to make an impact on the patent it is time to get into some classical sympathetic magic techniques to bring about a change. However you should always bare in mind what was told to the patent by the Goddess. The fact there was not a successful cure does not mean that what was suggested by the goddess was wrong. It might mean the patent does not believe it is possible without some form of rite taking place.

The Slaying of Apep

Take a piece of paper and draw a large serpent on it. Write the name of the illness in hieroglyphic (see the appendix) on the snake's belly. Attach the piece of paper around the patent's left arm with sticky tape .

Turn to the East and say:

> "Homage to thee, oh thou who art Re when thou Risest
> And Temu when thou settest.
> Thou Risest, Thou, Shinest,
> Thou who art the king of Gods.
> Thou Art the Lord of the Earth
> You are the creator of all those who live in the heights and the depths."

(face the patent)

> Re has journeyed to the point of darkness and there is great danger in the land. The rule of Maat is overthrown and conflict is where peace shall be and chaos is where there is law. The serpent of Apep raises his head of death, chaos and darkness and coils about <the name of the patent>

Draw the eye of Heru above the paper[2]

> "With the eye of Heru do I dazzle him with the brilliance of the sun and trap him with the spear of light.

> Get thee back fiend, before the darts of Re's beams.
> Re hath overthrown thy words.
> The gods have turned thy face backwards
> The Lynx has torn open thy breast
> The scorpion Goddess has cast fetters on thee
> Maat hath set forth thy destruction.
> Those who are in the path of truth have overthrown thee
> The Gods of the North, South, East and West have fettered thee.
> Thou art no more."

Tell the patent to take off the paper, spit on it and cast it into the fire. Tell them to say at the same time:

> "As Apep dies in the flames, so shall my illness be destroyed with him"

---

[2] The more traditional way was to make the serpent out of clay and then later have the patent crush it underfoot.

You say:

"Thus is evil smitten with the Knives of Heru. Thus evil is burned in the fires of Light. Be ye accursed Apep by all the names thou art known. Be thou accused in thy name Nesht as you are in Tutu. May the schemes of Hau-Hra come to naught as those of Kharubu the four times wicked. For as the flames destroy Apep, so it shall happen to the sons of Apep, and all who give him aid. There plans shall be confused for now and ever more."

Spell for General Healing

This is what is commonly called an auric sealing, it strengthens the physical body. The spell comes from the Book of the Dead . In your sacred space, stand behind the patent. Place your right hand on their right shoulder and left hand on their left. Assume the Goddess Het-Hor. Allow her energy to move down the right side of the person's body and up the left, then over the left side of the head and then to the right hand. Breath and drive energy along this circuit of force. Then say:

Ausar knows the names of your ka,
Nourishing ka,
ka of food,
lordly ka,
ka the ever-present helper,
ka which is a pair of kas begetting more kas,
healthy ka,
sparkling ka,
victorious ka,
ka the strong,
ka that strengthens the sun each day to rise from the world of the dead,
ka of shining resurrection,
powerful ka,
Effective ka.

Now place your right hand on the person's heart and left on their back immediately behind it. Allow her energy to move down the front of the person's body, to the feet and up the back, then over the head and then down the fact to the right hand. Breath and drive energy along this circuit of force. Repeat spell.

Illnesses of the four sons of Heru

The four sons of Heru, Amset, Duamutef, Hapi and Qebhsenuef have a special place in the healing process. As part of the mummification process, these four sons each looked after the unembalmed parts of the body. Although obviously these organs were important in physical life, in the afterlife divine energies replaced them. The old organs were sealed in jars with the head of a son of Heru on them. This was because the remains had a link to the new spiritual organs and still needed magical protection.

Amset was a mummified man. He was the protector of the liver of the deceased. Duamutef was a jackal. He was the protector of the stomach of the deceased. Hapi was a baboon. He was the protector of the lungs. Qebhsenuef was a falcon. He was the protector of the intestines. Illnesses to any of these parts of the body can be countered by the assumption of one of these godforms. A statue of the godform can be placed over the patent and held for five minutes while vibrating the name of the god. This causes aligning those parts of the body to the correct divine image.

Energy healing

In the 20th century of our own era it has become recognised that many healing systems are based either directly or in directly on the current flow of energy through-out the body. These ideas come from India where energy centers that control the various spiritual bodies is an important feature of the Indian energy techniques in Tantra.

There has been a belief that many of the beliefs of India came from Egypt first. Some of the more obvious symbols, such as the lotus, have fertilised both cultures. Some argue that Tantra makes up

Healing and Magic

the continuation of the original Indian aboriginal tradition which predates the coming of the Indo-European Aryan invaders and their Vedic religion (2000BC).

We do now that in later times the Egyptians and Indians traded with each other so it is possible there was a cross fertilisation of ideas. It is tempting to believe that some of the yogic and tantric ideas that have entered our own century might have their roots in Ancient Egypt. Unfortunately most tantric writings only start around the 4th century so we can't prove it. However, as I pointed out in the previous chapter, some of the beings identified in the Egyptian underworld present a symbolic template of creating physical bodies by energy systems that are remarkably similar to those of tantra. It does not take much to adjust these to create a full energy system of healing.

First this system is based on an idea of nine important energy centers at the base of the spine, groin, Navel, Solar Plexus, heart, throat, base of the back of the head, between the eyes and immediately above the head.

In the seventh division of the Duat we met nine beings who were responsible for bringing dead things to life. These were the spiritual channels behind the nine forms. They are like straws that allow divine energy to flow into the body. The Gods that are in charge of these spiritual channels are:

Hetep-Ta (base of the spine),
Amon (groin),
Sesheta-Baiu (navel),
Sekhen-Khaibit, (solar plexus),
Neb-Er-Tcher (heart),
Mennu (throat),
Mathenu (back of the head)
Metrui, (between the eyes)
Peremu (above the head).

These gods provide an electrical framework through which all energy flows around the body. If one of these straws is blocked or damaged energy leaks out and is unable to flow into the main centre.

In the Ninth division of the Duat the centers are activated by nine other beings who energise them with divine powers. The centers then begin to spin and energise the network built by the Gods of the Seventh division. These God names are Sekhti (at the base of the spine), Am-Sekhet-F (groin), Nehebeti (navel), Tchamuti (solar plexus), Neb-Aatti (heart), Heq-Neteru-F (throat), Pan-Ari (back of the head), Teser-Ari (Between the eyes) and Aha-Sekhet (The crown). If the centers are spinning too fast, or slowly then a person will suffer physical ill effects.

The nine centers in the East are called Chakras. Each centre is like a vortex that stores and shares energy through all seven of the bodies. Each centre is a specialised manufacturer of an effect on the personality. There are hundreds of these centers, but in this system there are only nine main ones.

They are visualised as being about the size of a large marble.

The Crown Centre

This is found a few inches above the head. It is responsible for mediating spiritual impulses to each of the seven bodies. On the positive side it can create an awareness of the spiritual reality behind everything. It is a source of creativity. When it becomes unbalanced it can create a loss of perspective and an inability to see reality, chronic exhaustion, depression, obsessional thinking and confusion. When it is too open and spinning too fast there is often a need to feel popular.

The Brow Centre

This is found between the eyes. It is responsible for mediating the forces of love, wisdom and creativity. When it is working properly it creates a person who is in touch with their feelings and can express them properly. Good teachers, healers and diplomats have often mastered the use of this centre. When it is unbalanced it leads to arrogance and a person who is overconfident. A person suffers from headaches or poor vision or mental illness. Nightmares and learning

Healing and Magic

difficulties and even hallucinations may result.

If you are a worrier, are scared of too many things, are over-sensitivity and belittling others often it signals this centre is firing too much

If you suffer from doubting, envy of others, and are forgetful all the time it suggests an underactive brow chakra.

The Back of the Head

It is found where the spine connects to the skull and the roof of the mouth. This has control over the nerves that advance from the brain to the different sense-organs. When it is working properly you have the ability to see, hear, taste, touch, and smell things that are there, rather than you think is there. It connects the spiritual realm with the higher aspects of the physical. When it is out of balance it leads to a mistaken understanding of the world around you and an inability to connect to the spiritual realm. If it is underactive it will lead to a total disconnection from the material world. This will eventually lead to depression and isolation. If it is overactive a person can become obsessed with sensual pleasures.

The Throat Centre

This is found in the centre of the throat. It is responsible for memory and understanding past events. It is the centre that becomes active when someone has a vision and is trying to apply it to reality. When it is unbalanced a person will become a perfectionist as a substitute for blocked creativity and an inability to express emotions. Domineering behaviour suggest an overactive throat chakra, while an under active or blocked chakra often shows stubbornness, depression and passiveness.

The Heart Centre

This centre is located around the physical heart. It is an important chakra because it mediates and balances the others.

Therefore if the heart centre is out of balance it is likely there is an imbalance in the other centers too. When this centre is working properly the person can nearly heal themselves, they become independent and self-confident.

If there is a problem with this centre the person often suffers from breathing problems high blood pressure, heart disease and some types of cancer. Emotionally a person might become paranoid and co-dependent. They will need constant confirmation of their self-worth from outside themselves, be possessive and dispassionate. If the centre becomes overactive a person will become full of rage and jealousy.

The Solar Plexus centre

This can be found at the soft point just below the central rib cage. It is the source of our personal power and self-will. It enables us to analyze the situation as it is now without worrying about past and present. A person who has this balanced is able to live for the moment and has a telepathic ability to work with their surrounding. It is this centre that is used a lot within martial arts and can create great feats of physical strength. If the centre is imbalanced a person will have a low sense of self-esteem, sometimes stomach ulcers and digestive problems, chronic fatigue, allergies and diabetes. If the centre is overactive a person can become judgmental and bullying. If it is blocked a person will feel isolated and fear trying anything new.

Navel

This can be found around the Navel. It is the source of Feelings received and Directly Experienced. It enables us to evaluating situations by what "Feels Right" and gut feelings. A person who has this centre balanced can make accurate decisions based on their intuition and not have to think too much about it. They can connect with other people on the Feeling level and feel centered and balanced. They are effective at expressing their feelings and are assertive. If it is overbalanced they can be overemotional, being ruled or swamped by your emotions and rational thought may be difficult. If it is out of balance they will often become co-dependant on another person and constantly look for guidance from others. If blocked people suffer from low vitality and can become picky or distracted.

Groin

This can be found between the navel and the genitals. It is the magnetic part of a person can draw others to a person. Effective politicians have a strongly developed sexual centre which is why they are able to draw others towards their points of view (it is why they get so involved in sex scandals). The powers of organised religion work through this centre. On a practical level it detoxifies the body.

If the centre is imbalanced a person will have an unbalanced sex drive, emotional instability and feelings of isolation. They may become powerless, frigid or suffer bladder and prostate problems and lower back pain.

When it is overactive a person will be arrogant, lustful and seek to dominate others. When the sex centre is under active, a person becomes mistrust of others, introvert and can't express their emotions.

The Base

This centre is at the base of the spine but is connected directly to another lesser centre at the balls of the feet. It is the job of this centre to connect to the spiritual energy and natural power that is stored in the earth. Its energy awakens and reawakens all the other centers.

When this base centre is blocked, a person will have poor self-confidence, be self-destructive and fretful, and find difficulty in achieving goals.

If it is overbalanced the individual will be self-centerd, materialistic, aggressive and impulsive.

Raising the Djed pillar

Having described the various energy bodies and the centers that power them we are not going to use various techniques to strengthen, balance and empower them.

Using these techniques it is possible to open the centers safely and balance them without having to do this. We do so indirectly using the magical tool of visualisation. Visualisation on a symbol of balance causes the centers to open and tune themselves correctly in a sympathetic reaction. It might be a little slower than of yoga that work with the centers, but it is a lot safer.

If done correctly these exercises will blow you head off. It is not to be done lightly as it can bring about the sorts of changes you do not want. The best way to approach it with a religious frame of mind, an idea that you are working with a higher being to bring about its will in your life and the universe. This prevents some of the problems of the Ba (such as neurosis) from inflaming and becoming crippling physical and mental illness.

The Ba is like a bank vault of a neurotic tendency you might have and these techniques bring out the big ones for you to face. They contain useful energy which is trapped and needs to be used if the ceremonial magician is to fulfill their destiny.

This creates amounts of etheric and astral energy within the subtle bodies and can cause specific changes of consciousness and hopefully personal transformation.

The Dejd pillar exercise helps ceremonial magicians to equilibrate the two contending forces. It provides a powerful unconscious call to live out the middle pillar within one's life as a flexible, just and balanced human. It calls us to live in the world rather than separate from it.

It uses divine names to strengthen and purify the astral body. It links our etheric and astral bodies into the great power sources of the universe. With regular use it has great benefits on the physical health and well-being of anyone who uses it regularly.

Stand in your sacred pace facing East. Stand straight and try to relax as much as possible. Perform the regulated breathing exercises of the previous chapter.

- Say: "I will raise up the Djed Pillar that Ausar may be reborn in earth."

Healing and Magic

- Take a deep breath and imagine a white ball of light above your head. See it expand and spin. Vibrate the name Peremu. This will create the form of a closed white lotus above your head. Do this six times or until you can see it clearly. Then picture white light pouring down from above you and filling the lotus flower until it opens and spins. Now vibrate the name Aha-Sekhet six times.

- Imagine the light flowing down to a closed white lotus between your eyes. Vibrate the name Metrui. This will create the form of a closed white lotus above your head. Do this six times or until you can see it clearly. Then imagine white light pouring down from above you and filling the lotus flower until it opens and spins. Now vibrate the name Teser-Ari six times.

- Imagine the light flowing down to a closed white lotus at the back of your head. Vibrate the name Mathenu. This will create the form of a closed white lotus above your head. Do this six times or until you can see it clearly. Then picture white light pouring down from above you and filling the lotus flower until it opens and spins. Now vibrate the name Pan-Ari six times.

- Imagine the light flowing down to a closed white lotus at the throat. Vibrate the name Mennu. This will create the form of a closed white lotus above your head. Do this six times or until you can see it clearly. Then picture white light pouring down from above you and filling the lotus flower until it opens and spins. Now vibrate the name Heq-Neteru-F six times.

- Imagine the light flowing down to a closed white lotus at the heart. Vibrate the name Neb-Er-Tcher. This will create the form of a closed white lotus above your head. Do this six times or until you can see it clearly. Then picture white light pouring down from above you and filling the lotus flower until it opens and spins. Now vibrate the name Neb-Aatti six times.

- Imagine the light flowing down to a closed white lotus solar plexus. Vibrate the name Sekhen-Khaibit. This will create the form of a closed white lotus above your head. Do this six times or until you can see it clearly. Then picture white light pouring down from above you and filling the lotus flower until it opens and spins. Now vibrate the name Tchamuti six times.

• Imagine the light flowing down to a closed white lotus at the navel. Vibrate the name Sesheta-Baiu. This will create the form of a closed white lotus above your head. Do this six times or until you can see it clearly. Then imagine white light pouring down from above you and filling the lotus flower until it opens and spins. Now vibrate the name Nehebeti six times.

• Imagine the light flowing down to a closed white lotus at the groin. Vibrate the name Amon. This will create the form of a closed white lotus above your head. Do this six times or until you can see it clearly. Then imagine white light pouring down from above you and filling the lotus flower until it opens and spins. Now vibrate the name Am-Sekhet-F six times.

• Imagine the light flowing down to a closed white lotus at the base of the spine. Vibrate the name Hetep-Ta. This will create the form of a closed white lotus above your head. Do this six times or until you can see it clearly. Then imagine white light pouring down from above you and filling the lotus flower until it opens and spins. Now vibrate the name Sekhti six times.

• Say: "Let that which has been dead ARISE. Breathe in and draw green light from the centre of the earth, through the feet, upwards through the centers starting with the base cente and moving upwards until you reach the crown.

• Breathe out and let this centre explode with white light that shower through your aura, cleaning and purifying it. Allow the light to gather at your feet and repeat the process 10 times

If you want you can finish with this invocation which is inspired by the pyramid texts while picturing the djed pillar built within your aura.

The head of [Insert your Name] is the head of Heru; I come forth and rise into heaven.
The skull of this [Insert your Name] is the Dekan star of the god; I come forth and rise into heaven.
The brow of [Insert your Name] is the brow of Nu; I come forth and rise into heaven.
The face of [Insert your Name] is the face of Up-uatu; I come forth and rise into heaven.
The eyes of [Insert your Name] are the eyes of the Great Lady, the first of the Souls of Anu; I come forth and rise into heaven.
The nose of [Insert your Name] is the nose of Tehuti; I come forth and rise into heaven.
The mouth of [Insert your Name] is the mouth of Khens-ur; I come forth, and rise into heaven.
The tongue of [Insert your Name] is the tongue of Maaa (Truth) in the Maat Boat; I come forth and rise into heaven.
The teeth of [Insert your Name] are the teeth of the Souls of [Anu]; I come forth and rise into heaven.
The lips of [Insert your Name] are the lips of Aset. I come forth and rise into heaven.
The chin of [Insert your Name] is the chin of Nest-khent-Sekhem (the throne of the First Lady of Sekhem); I come forth and rise into heaven.
The thighbone of [Insert your Name] is the thighbone of the Bull Sma; I come forth and rise into heaven.
The shoulders of [Insert your Name] are the shoulders of Set; I come forth and rise into heaven.
The two thighs of [Insert your Name] are the two thighs of Heqet; I come forth and rise into heaven.
The buttocks of [Insert your Name] are like the Semktet Boat and the Mantchet Boat; I come forth and rise into heaven.
The legs of [Insert your Name] are the legs of Net (Neith) and Serqet; I come forth and rise into heaven.
The knees of [Insert your Name] are the knees of the twin Souls who are at the head of Sekhet-Tcher; I come forth and rise into heaven.

The soles of [Insert your Name] are like the Maati Boat; I come forth and rise into heaven.
The toes of [Insert your Name] are the toes of the Souls of Anu; I come forth and rise into heaven.
[Insert your Name] is a god, the son (or daughter) of a god; I come forth and rise into heaven.
[Insert your Name] is the son (or daughter) of Re, who loves him; I come forth and rise into heaven.
Re hath sent forth [Insert your Name]; I come forth and rise into heaven.
Re hath begotten [this] [Insert your Name]; I come forth and rise into heaven.
Re hath given birth to [Insert your Name]; I come forth and rise into heaven.

Magical spells

Over the years I have built up several magical rituals which might be useful for would-be Egyptian shamans to try out. Obviously, by being a walker between the worlds, you will come up with your own series of charms and spells to play with. These are just to give you an idea. They are inspired by the pyramid texts unless I say otherwise

To protect a house

Assume the godform of Heru and walk around the house:
In the centre of the house say:
'*I have come; I have dedicated this house to <insert name of home owner>*'

In the hallways:
'*Purer is this broad-hall than Aset .*'

At each door
'*At this door (or, entrance) is an obelisk; the door is double (that is with two leaves), and is sealed with two eyes Let not evil enter. Do not open to him your arms. Let him be gone at once. Let not Heru*

> come in this his evil coming. Do not open your arms to that which is evil and will do harm.
> Let not Set come in this his evil coming; do not open to him your arms; that which comes in his name. Let him go to the Duart at once. Let him go to the lake of fire.
> If the unbalanced come, do not open your arms.
> If the evil spirits come, do not open your arms.
> If the gods come in malice, do not open your arms.
> If <the home owner> and his friends and family Open your arms.
> In each room draw the eye of Heru
> Pure is this eye of Heru, let evil and darkshadows flee away. Let the eye rest here.

Return to the centre of the house

> They who put a finger against this house of <homeowner> shall be putting a finger against the house of Heru. May Nebt-Het and Aset go against him. He will be without support, his house will be without support; He is accursed; he is one who eats his (own) body.

A BLESSING

This is for the general well-being of a person. The godstick of Ram or Hawk should touch the object as the following is said. The God should be seen to wrap its arms, or wings, about the object being blessed.

> Almighty Ram (or Hawk) make < person being blessed > endure; as the name of Atum, chief of the Great Ennead, endures.
> As the name of Shu endures so may <the name of person being blessed>. endure,
> May his or her house endure forever and ever.
> As the name of Tefnut is established, so may <the name of person being blessed> be established,
> As the name of Geb, the soul of the earth, endures, so may <the name of person being blessed> endure.
> As the name of Ausar, in Abydos, endures so may <the name of

person being blessed> endure
As the name of Re, on the horizon, endures, so may <the name of person being blessed> endure.

Rite of Skrying

Take an earthen bowl. Paint the inside black. In sacred space say:

Oh you who art Het-Hor. Grant me a vision of <whatever you want to see> Quickly? Put light and in my vessel. Open to me the earth, open to me the Duart, open to me the abyss, Open the view to the gods that are in heaven, that are exalted. Come mighty Het-Hor put light in my vessel.

Fill the bowl with pure olive oil.

This vessel-divination is the vessel-divination of Aset, when she sought the limbs of Ausar. Come in to me and cause my eyes to be opened to them all. For I am the Lion King. I am the Ram King, Ram-lion-lotus is my name. I am the gryphon of the shrine of the Great God. Beautiful Oxherd, my leader Het-Hor. I ask thee about here to-day: and do thou cause my eyes to be opened. Protect me as I bend down over this bowl. Geb, lord of earth help me. I am Hor-Amon that sitteth at this vessel-divination here to-day. As I speak with the Ancestors, with the Gods, may there be Maat in my Eyes, Maat in my ears and Maat in my mouth.

Rite of Spiritual development after a time of trouble

This is designed to help you gain a spiritual experience during those moments after trouble. It is designed to help a person break out of a rut, or a period where everything get worse. Each person will receive whatever they are capable then but often this rite has been a way of reminding yourself of your spiritual path. Ideally this ceremony should be performed close to Noon outdoors in the sunshine.

In sacred space you should get yourself into a trance by chanting the name Ausar and assuming his godform.

The after a pause you should say:

I am like Ausar, reassembled and ready to ascend to the throne of the stars.
I have been found perfected by the Gods by Trial and yet my heart has remained fast.
My soul is ready to stand among the gods as Heru who lives in Trw.
May terror come into being in the hearts of the gods.
I shall lay hold of the Imperishable stars, our bones shall not perish, my flesh will not sicken.
I shall walk among the Gods.
Imagine yourself getting onto Re's boat and sailing with the Sun into the heavens.
As you get higher in the heavens say:
The doors of the sky are open to me the doors of the starry sky are thrown open for me for I have gone down as the jackal.
The great cosmic mother has placed her hands on me for there is no mother among humanity who could bear us and no father who could have begotten us. My mother is the great wild cow Het-Hor.
My seat is among the Gods. Re leans on me.
My scent is the scent of the gods.
I am bound to the morning star, born as the moon, Re lifts me to the horizon.
The Imperishable stars follow me.
I traverse the sky with Orion, we navigate the netherworld with Ausar, I rise from the East, we are renewed with each season, and reborn.
I am Ausar who rises the sky in peace. My mother Nut is welcoming me because I have returned to our rightful place in peace. She says to us that we have returned of our own free will to our new responsibilities and evil has not touched us on our journey. She will not allow us to fall and not allow us to slip back.
I climb the primal hill of the land amid the sea which is ruled by none. Shu is below our feet. We live on what he lives on and we pass our limits.
The doors of the sky are open to us and we enter the house of Heru. Any god that helps me shall endure forever and shall rise with me.

Any god that shall not take me to heaven shall be forgotten.

Take a deep breath and Vibrate the name Re. Imagine yourself as merging with the sun at noon.

Chapter Nine

The Shaman Alone

Modern neo-pagans commemorate festivals and other religious observances as part of their spiritual tradition. This usually means celebrating the equinoxes and solstices. While Egypt did not celebrate these times of the year they did make good use of festivals. These were held on certain days sacred to a God, Goddess, Totem or ancestor. When temple culture became settled, after our period, this involved a statue of the God or Goddess being taken on a boat ride or in a procession outside the temple. This was mostly just to show the power of the Gods to the people and allow them to bask in the energy of the God or Goddess they were supporting. Other times the myths of the various gods or goddess would be acted out. Sometimes these rites would be conducted partly or entirely in public, sometimes in secret. Our Egyptian shaman would have been unlikely to have performed such elaborate rites. However, these festivals might have been born out of his commemoration ceremonies.

It is up to you to decide what these festivals mean to you (if anything). For example it would be largely pointless to commemorate the annual flooding of the Nile because it doesn't do that any more and you do not depend on it to raise your grain or cattle. However, you can commemorate the flood as symbolically. You could use it to call on the gods to give you abundance, money, food, for the rest of the year.

July Season of Flood – Ruled by Thoth – (Ibis totem)
1st Birthday of Ra-Horakhty (Hawk Totem)

15th Offerings to Hapy and Amun to secure a good flood (prosperity for the year)
19th Festival of Thoth
20th Tekh Festival of Drunkenness
22nd Great Procession of Osiris

August Menkhet
15th Ipet festival as 11-day festivities for Amun (Ram)
18th Khnum and Anuqet,
27th Two-day local festival of Mont
28th Festival of Satet and Anuqet,

September Hathor
9th festival for Amun
30th Festival of Anuqet.

October Nehebkau
1st festival for Hathor (Cow)
18th Osiris myth enacted including the Plowing the Earth, Sokar festival and the raising the Djed-pillar

November Season of Sowing
1st festival of Nehebkau
20th festival of Wadjyt,
29th festival of Bast (cat)
30th festival of Shesmet

December Rekehwer
1st festival of Anubis
30th Amun-in-the-festival-of-raising-heaven' a midwinter rite where creating the universe was commemorated.

February Rekehnedjes
1st festival of Ptah

March Paenrenenutet
4th festival of Bast (cat) Worshipers of the cat totem must eat onions!
25th harvest offering to Renenutet
27th granary offering to Renenutet

April Season of Summer Paenkhons
1st festival of Renenutet, and birthday of Nepri (personification of grain)
10th adoration of Anubis
11th festival of Min
May Khentkhety
Festival of the Valley celebrated at the New Moon (ancestors)
June Ipet-hemet
15th Offerings to Hapy and Amun to secure a good flood
30th festival of Hathor (Cow)

Every few years the Egyptians added five days onto the calendar so their lunar calendars would not be out of wack with the progression of the Sun. These worked a bit like a leap year in our modern calendar. Each of these five days was dedicated to the birthday of each of the following gods and goddesses. Day 1 Osiris, day 2 Horus, day 3 Seth, day 4 Isis, and day 5 Nephthys. It is difficult to work these days into a modern calendar so I do all five on the same day – the gods and goddesses do not mind. I think as you get older you forget your own birthdays anyway.

There is nothing to stop you building your own ritual calendar, just so long as you stick to it. In fact because we do not know when the local festivals were for different gods and goddesses you will have to do something like that anyway.

The purpose of such regular worship, if any is needed, is to deepen your personal relationship with the Gods and Goddesses. This will give you a sense of a place in the universe, which is sadly lacking in modern times. It will give you a space to meet the spiritual forces behind the universe under a human face that you can respect. Most of the Egyptian Gods were a lot more friendly than many of the more recent monotheistic creations and can form bonds that are remarkably like friendship. Of course the Ancient Egyptians didn't see them like that, their approach was much more practical and literal. One of the advantages of the monotheists is that in the last two thousand years they have encouraged a personal relationship with there gods. There is no reason the Egyptian Gods cannot be approached in a similar mystical way, and many are.

Initiation

There is no doubt in my mind that Egyptian society would have had ritualised initiations. Many of these would be ceremonies that marked the passage of time and aging. For example, a boy or girl would probably have some form of rite of passage ceremony when they reached puberty. What these rites were, we have no idea. It is also likely that shamans and priests would have undergone some grueling initiations before they were considered worthy to hold that role.

In modern times initiation, while perhaps owing much to the later systems of Egyptian temple worship, means something different. It usually means a ceremony where someone is inducted into a group. The term comes from Freemasonry and has little to interest us here. However the term also has a deeper spiritual meaning.

According to the esoteric writers Chic & Sandra Tabatha Cicero, initiation is the passage into a distinctly new existence following spiritual growth.

> *"The earmarks of this spiritual "new birth" are indicated by an expansion of the mind to include a realisation of higher levels of consciousness. Initiation is the forerunner of immortality. It is that which gives us the ability to explore the Divine within us. Humanity has always had the potential for immortality, but only acquires It when men and women affiliate themselves with the immortal spiritual substance that supports all facets of the physical universe; that same Divine quintessence which is far too often neglected by the general public."*

While walking on the shamanic path you will experience flashes of insight after which nothing can ever be the same again. The various techniques described in this book will, as gradually as an unfolding Lotus, awaken you to your superhuman potential. The word initiation means "to begin." It is the beginning of a new stage of life. The modern Egyptian shaman is looking for an initiation every day.

They are seeking to achieve this by fusing their lives into the nature that surrounds them and the spirits that live within their interior universes.

So, despite the temptation, I did not write any initiation ceremonies into this book, even though it is likely that they did take place in Pre-dynastic Egypt. Instead I have written ceremonies that can lead to different forms of initiation.

Therefore, I have placed an emphasis on understanding and working with the God Re. Although his worship was strong in Pre-dynastic times, some think he is a Mesopotamian god with an Egyptian Hawk's headed mask. . If he was a foreign god, he was so substantially made Egyptian that it is impossible to see him as belonging to somewhere else anyway. Not that it matters, it is just easier to see the divine spirit that shows through initiation as a sun.

Dion Fortune's magical order the Society of Inner Light used to open their rituals with the phrase "from those who see the light of the Most High face unto face I bring you greetings". The idea was the sun was an expression of the secret and holy god that we see face-to-face each day and yet fail to notice. The first initiation of a shaman is going to happen when they to notice that for the first time.

Shamans in Groups

I have not written any group workings for Egyptian shamans. The path of a shaman is always lonely. It is hard to find cases of groups of Shamans gathering regularly, because each has a spontaneous way of working. A shaman's work is a lot more individualistic and contains its own symbolic language. Although it is possible to share that, even train people in its use, it is almost too unique to do this. Although the Egyptian shamans are more structured than their cousins in Siberia or Native America , the spontaneous, ecstatic method of a shaman does not work within a group environment. There should be nothing strange about this. The role of a shaman is a hybrid of a doctor and an artist. How often do you see groups of them working together?

There is one exception to this. This is when a shaman has a congregation who help him in performing a particular working. In this circumstance, the shaman acts in a similar position to an Indian Guru. A group of people, of various levels of experience, help him in the working, by chanting or playing instruments but they are directed by the shaman.

As I said in my book, 'Gathering the Magic', this circle is a huge test for the ego of the Shaman. However, it is a way that people can have spiritual experiences in a safe controlled environment.

Nearly ten years ago I was involved in a Shamanic style group that was focused on one experienced teacher figure. The methods used were similar to what we used here, although there was a stronger Native American overtone to the proceedings. The rite involved sitting in a circle, in the pitch-black, listening to a drumbeat. We would usually go on a spirit journey.

Once one of the students brought a Native American shaker which he had just bought to show the teacher. The teacher was talking to me at the time and there was no one else in the room. He decided it would be a good idea to put the shaker in the middle of the circle to "give the spirits something to shake".

We started the ritual and put out the lights. We were meeting at night in an old farmhouse in the middle of nowhere. It was so dark the air was like treacle. Everyone held hands and the drumbeat started and soon everyone was chanting away. The shaker in the middle of the room started to rattle. It was as if it had been picked up and was being shaken. I assumed the teacher had stood up and gone and shaken it. So, ever the sceptic, I rolled my legs underneath the rattling shaker. I moved my feet around and realised that for me not to have kicked anyone with my legs the shaker would have to be hanging in midair. It was still too dark to see so I returned to my position in the circle and carried on with the working. As the vision quest closed down, the shaker rattled slowly to the ground and stopped.

No one but me and the owner of the rattle, who was playing the drum throughout the ritual, knew why the teacher had placed it in the centre of the circle. As the lights came up, I still assumed that somehow the teacher had stood up in the rite to pay the shaker and avoid my sceptical feet. In a guru based group, which was what this one was, no one would dare move other than the teacher[1]. Touching magical equipment was a no-no. However the woman sitting next to the teacher complained "That is the last time I sit next to you in a circle, you held my hand so tightly, throughout the whole ritual, I have pins and needles."

Group shamanic workings can create some of these effects, but on the shamanic path it can be a problem and a distraction to your work. Also the work of a shaman is exhaustive, in a way that is a little difficult for those who are only taking a passive role can guess at. A real working can last for hours, well above the boredom pain threshold of a group. When it is over, the group will want to socialise, while the shaman will be looking for something more relaxing such as a coma.

So, although I am a great fan of magical groups, I do not think they are a part of this path.

A Shaman alone

As part of your work you should endeavor to do something connected with your path daily. Initially this will be difficult as much of the work needs you to be self-motivated. Every aspect of your personality that wants things to stay the same will rebel. If you try to do the ceremonies to the sun every morning there will be something that will go wrong and you will forget. You should just persist until it all becomes a habit. Don't try to do too much too quickly. Such make slow steps and you might catch your lower self off guard and it might become a habit before it knows what has happened.

Try to do the energy workings at least once a month. Until you have done this for a few years you should not try to do it daily. It will take a while for your ba to be able to take the energy.

You should try to write down your experiences and analyze

---
[1] I think it is clear I have authoritiy 'issues'.

them intellectually. When you are working by yourself, you need to develop some excellent discrimination over your experiences. If, because your experiences, you become convinced that you are meant to rule the world, or be some great spiritual teacher, or become the messiah, it is a good time to give it all a rest for a while. This is called ego inflation and it needs to be watched carefully, as it carries off some good shaman.

When you want to create new ceremonies you can adapt them from the rituals that have been found from in the Coffin, Pyramid texts, the book of the Dead, or other Egyptian rituals that have been published. Most of the early translations are considered public domain and can be found on the Internet. Although modern Egyptologists might consider the translations of Wallace Budge a little old hat now, they are good enough for you.

However you should rewrite everything so it means something to you. As I said in my book Magical Pathworking Sacred texts were written in a different era and another language and lose much in translation. It is impossible to know exactly what the Ancient Egyptians meant when they wrote some of the lines from the Pyramid texts. For example the phrase "may you not moan like a cedar" sounds a little strange to modern ears. Cedars don't moan much more than any other tree, so unless there was a legend attached to cedars that we have since lost, it is meaningless. However we could still use the line by saying "may you not moan like a wind whistling through the cedar" could be OK.

A ceremony should have a clear purpose. This is easy when you are doing a rite of healing or something similar because you will know what the aim is. It becomes more difficult when you find yourself a good piece of Egyptian text and you want to turn it into a ritual. Let's use a paraphrased example from Utterence 505 from the Pyramid texts.

> "Isis is before me and Nebt-Het is behind me, Wepwawet opens a way for me, Shu lifts me up, the Souls of On set up a stairway for me to reach the Above, and Nut puts her hand on me just as she did for Osiris on the day when he died."

Let us look for clues about what we can do with this. First it is called an ascension text, which means it is something that represents the dead king, or living shaman, being raised up into a spiritual state.

First let us look at the obvious. The person is being led upwards by Wepwawet into a new spiritual state. This spiritual action is caused by a ceremony involving the polarity between goddesses Isis and Nebt-Het. The power for the ceremony is provided by Shu and the souls of On provide the ritual framework.

So first we have to find out what these various beings represent. Wepwawet is the 'opener of the ways' a spiritual guide. Aset and Nebt-Het are the light and dark mothers involved in the resurrection of Osiris. Shu was the god of air. He is seen as separating the Sky and the Earth. The souls of On are the Eight gods of Iunu, that embodied the creative source and chief forces of the universe. Nut is the sky goddess.

So here we have many sky images here, which is not surprising given the ceremony was an ascension into the sky.

In all rituals work out what you want to imagine. Visualisation should encompass the spiritual direction that you want to go. In this case, we want to build a ladder to the stars and be helped up it by the Gods and Goddesses.

Next, we need to see what ritual techniques we will use. Godform assumption of Osiris would be logical and Shu's involvement suggests there should be an emphasis on breathing.

Then there is a matter of working out the words that will help you ascend. These are up to you and I suggest you keep them as short as possible. In the shamanic tradition it is better to repeat short things many times, than it is to do a single long speech.

So here is my version of rite:

The star ladder

In your sacred space, lie flat, on your back and assume the godform of Osiris. Say:

"I would ascend to the stars on a ladder of light.
"I am Osiris. Isis is at my head, Nebt-Het is at my feet"

Repeat the last line until you can see and feel the Goddesses, their wings outstretched above your body. Now breath slowly and evenly bringing light from above your head down to your feet and back up again. Do this for several minutes. Then as you breathe out say "Light Mother awaken me" and you breathe in say "Dark Mother awaken me" Do this until you are ready to ascend.

In your mind's eye stand up and visualise a tall ladder leading up to the sky. KEEP BREATHING!

Go to the ladder. See before you the Jackal Wepwawet climb the ladder before you. Chant the names of the eight primal Gods of On as you step up the ladder into the sky

Kerhet (night), take a step
then chant the name Kerh (night), take another step
chant Kekiut (obscurity), take another step
chant kekiu (obscurity), take another step
chant Hehut (Eternity), take another step
chant Hehu (Eternity), take another step
chant Nut (night), take another step
chant Nu (night)

Standing on top of the ladder, with the earth below you say:

"I merge into my Mother Nut.
I am a creature of the stars"

Allow yourself time to experience what this will do to you. It is a heavy ritual. Once you have finished, imagine yourself climbing down the ladder, into your sacred space and take some time to 'earth' yourself.

The Way is Open

The shaman was an important part of village life in Pre-dynastic Egypt. They were doctor, priest, teacher, counselor, magical protector and guide to the underworld. Modern shamans are unlikely to be able to achieve the social significance in our modern society, but that does not mean the role is no longer needed. There have to be those who are prepared to walk between the worlds and live on the edges of the realms of imagination and 'reality'. Those who use their powers to heal, to help others move from one realm to another and to be a living expression of the gods.

We live in a 'pick and mix' age where occultists select the bits they want from a system and move onto another. While there is nothing wrong with gaining this experience, you have to take a spiritual system seriously enough to weave it into the fabric of your life.

Egyptian shamanism has much going for it in that regard. It is a pantheistic religion that finds unity in diversity. It uses animals and plants to anchor you into the real world, it recognizes the power of the Ancestors in your life, and the tribal links you might have. Finally it provides a symbolic alphabet with which you can explore the uncharted realms of inner space.

But for it to have its effect, it calls on you to work it; to meet with its Gods and Goddesses and to walk in its symbolism as much as possible.

It is a life built on worship of the forces of nature, mind and emotions as God. Postmodern society has lost what it means to worship. Worship is the commitment to a God or Goddess or even a pantheon of them believing that in them you will see flashes of the reality that transcends both you and them. Worship is a relationship with the Divine symbols that direct our lives.

A true Egyptian shaman starts his or her day by worshipping the Re as he emerges from the Duart. He is not worshipping a ball of gas, but as a symbol of that invisible energy through which we live and move and have our being, emerging into consciousness.

Try for a week getting up at Sunrise (it is easier if you try this in winter). Stand outside as the sun starts to push his way into the sky and say:

Hail, you Re the lord of rays, who risest on the horizon.
Shine with your beams of light on my face

For I sing praise to you at dawn,
May I rise with you this day and come forth with thee into heaven
May I set with thee in the Matet Boat in the morning.
May I cleave my path among the stars of heaven with thee.
Which never rest.
Hail to thee, O Heru-khuti, who art the god Khepera, the self-created.
When thou risest on the horizon and sheddest thy beams of light on the Lands of the South and of the North,
thou art beautiful, yea beautiful,
And all the gods rejoice when they behold thee, the king of heaven.
The god Thoth is stablished in the bows of thy boat to destroy all thy foes.
And I, come into thy presence, so I may be with thee,
And may behold thy Disk every day.
Let me be made new in by thy presence
Let me arrive in the Land of Eternity,
Let me enter the Land of Everlastingness.
Let me see thee in all things I do this day.

Sunset should also be a time of worship. It is the moment when the consciousness enters the Duart and casts its healing rays upon that which is hurt, or illuminates secret wisdom. So at sunset you should watch Re enter the underworld and say:

Send forth light, O Mountain!
Let radiance arise from that which hath devoured Re
For as Re enters the darkness of the Duart
May he bring his light to the hidden places
May he bring his light to the Ancestors
May he bring his light to the depths of humanity's soul
May he slay Apep and be reborn in the place of greatest darkness
May he ascend anew in the Eastern Horizon as Kephra the self created
Hail to thee oh Re
Thy servant awaits your rebirth.

Becoming an Egyptian shaman is a way of life, and for that matter, death. It is not simply collecting a few Egyptian statues or wearing a fake leopard skin. It is a process of awakening those symbols, which were held sacred for thousands of years, inside you. A person who is able to realise this goal is truly a Sem Priest; a walker between the worlds forever.

Appendix
Egyptian Hieroglyphics

If you get deeper into the path of being an Egyptian Shaman you might which to use Egyptian Hieroglypics to make you talismans and to mark your implements. It is not too important as the path of the Pre-dynastic shaman pre-dates that of writing. However it would give your work an authentic and mysterious feel. Writing was the gift of Thoth to the Egyptians and was always considered a sacred and exclusive task.
was considered.
Without actually learning Ancient Egyptian words, which would be beyond all but the most enthusastic, it is possible to get the feel of using Hieroglyhics by transliterating the latin letters into their nearest Hieroglyhic letter. Below is a simplified Hierogyphic alphabet to get you started.

English	Egyptian
A	
B	
Ch	
D	
E	
F	
G	

English	Egyptian
H	⌼
I	ᚏ
J	ꜣ
K	◡
L	𓃀
M	𓅓
N	〜
O	☥
P	⊖
Q	△
R	◯
S	⎮
T	◠
U	Use W
V	Use F
W	𓅱
X	◡ ⎮
Y	𓏭

English	Egyptian
Z	—⊚—

ABOUT THE AUTHOR

NICK FARRELL has been initiated into six different traditions which have their roots in the Golden Dawn. His first group was *BUILDERS OF THE ADYTUM* in New Zealand. Later he worked with former members of the last Golden Dawn temple to close its doors, *Whare Ra*, in New Zealand and is a member of the still thriving side order, the *ORDER OF THE TABLE ROUND*. He moved to the United Kingdom and for many years followed Dion Fortune's *INNER LIGHT* tradition. Later he joined Chic Cicero's *HERMETIC ORDER OF THE GOLDEN DAWN*, helping that order to establish itself in the United Kingdom.

In 2009, he founded the *MAGICAL ORDER OF THE AURORA AUREA* which follows the Golden Dawn system. It is an International Order based in Rome with a correspondence course and temples working within the Golden Dawn tradition being established across the World.

More information can be found on the Order's website www.auroraaurea.com or on his own website www.nickfarrell.eu.